Scott Foresman

Phonics Workbook

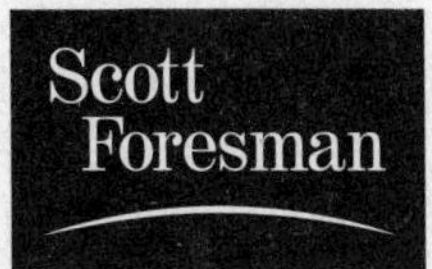

Editorial Offices: Glenview, Illinois • Parsippany, New Jersey • New York, New York
Sales Offices: Parsippany, New Jersey • Duluth, Georgia • Glenview, Illinois
Carrollton, Texas • Ontario, California

ISBN 0-328-02432-5

10-V034-060504

Name ______________________________

 Circle.

1. 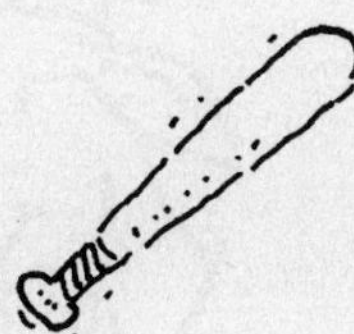  

2. 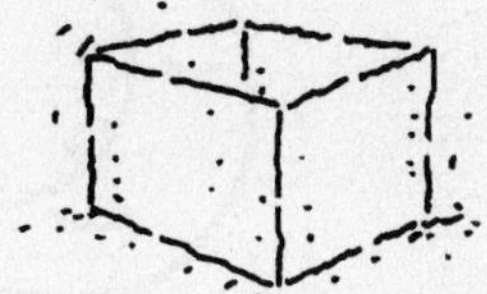  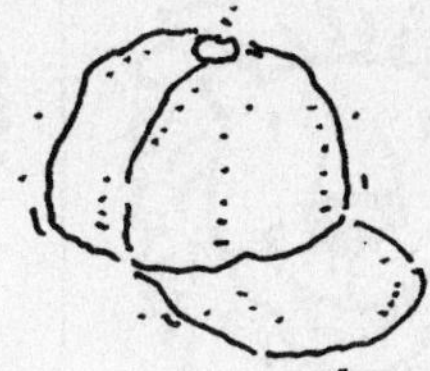

3. 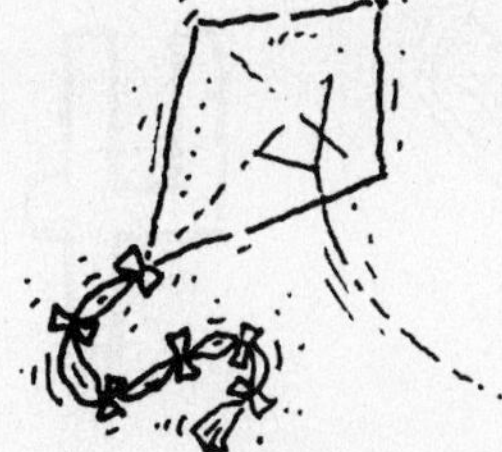  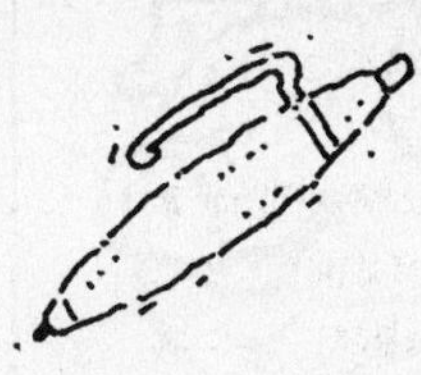

4.   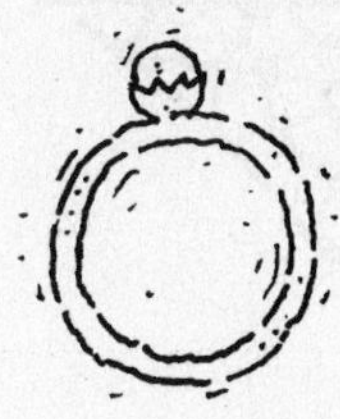

5.   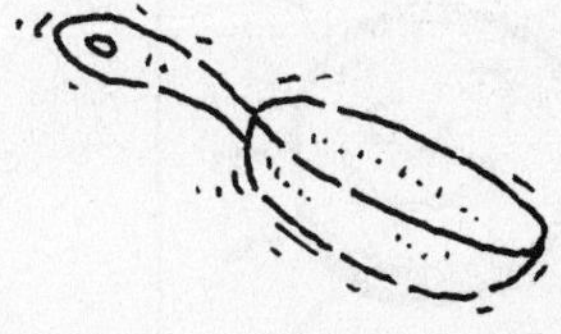

 **Directions:** In each row, circle the pictures that rhyme.

 **Home Activity:** Read nursery rhymes and help your child find rhyming words.

Name ______________________

Circle.

1\.  |   

2\.  |   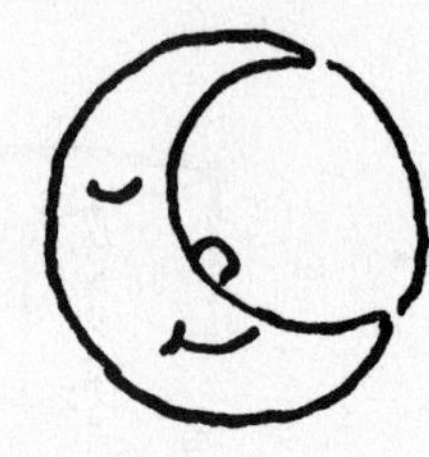

3\.  |  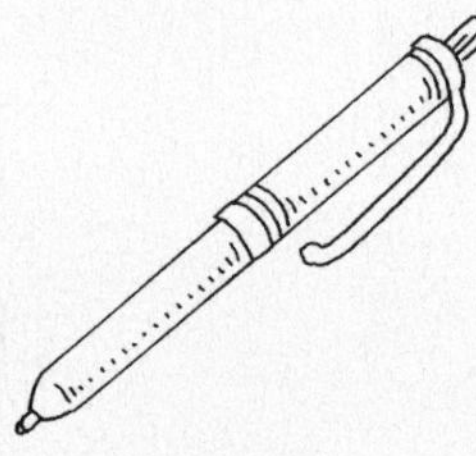 

4\. 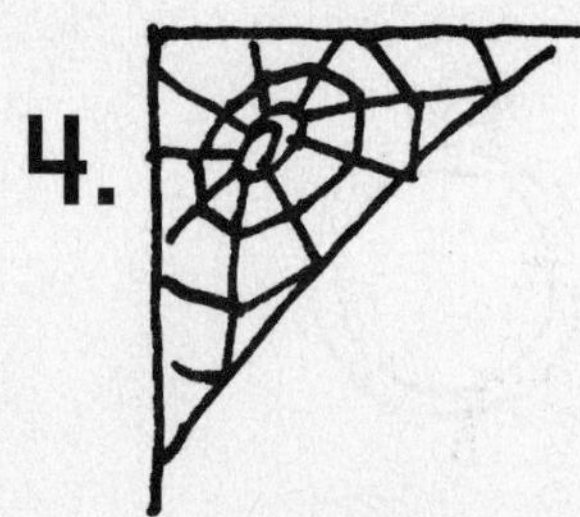 |   

5\.  |   

Directions: In each row, circle the picture that begins with the same sound as the first picture.

Home Activity: Help your child find things in your home that begin alike.

Name ______________________

Circle.

M	A	M
J	J	O
D	G	D
A	R	A

Directions: Circle the letter that matches the first letter.

Home Activity: Point to letters and ask your child to name them.

Name ______________________

Circle.

m	m	n
d	t	d
j	g	j
a	c	a

Directions: Circle the letter that matches the first letter.

Home Activity: Name letters on this page. Have your child point to them and repeat the letter names.

Name ______________________________

Aa Bb Cc Dd Ee Ff Gg Hh Ii
Jj Kk Ll Mm Nn Oo Pp Qq Rr
Ss Tt Uu Vv Ww Xx Yy Zz

Write.

Mrs. Greene

Juan

Mary

Directions: Write your name on the line. Use the alphabet as a guide.

Home Activity: Have your child name the letters in his or her name.

Name ______________________________

Draw.

1\.

2\.

3\.

4\.

Directions: Draw a picture of something that rhymes with the picture in the row.

Home Activity: Say two rhyming words (*cat—hat*) and ask your child to name other words that rhyme.

Name ________________________

Color.

1.

2.

3.

4.

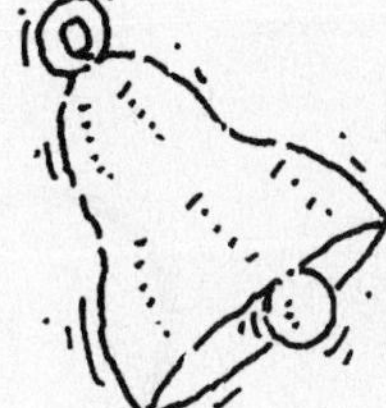

Directions: In each box, color the pictures that begin with the same sound.

Home Activity: Point to and name an item in your home. Have your child say a word that begins with the same sound.

Name ______________________

Circle.

T	T	K	L
B	L	B	C
R	R	G	P
Y	W	Y	A
G	G	T	U

Directions: Circle the letter that matches the first letter.

Home Activity: Point to each letter and have your child say the letter name.

Name ______________________________

Circle.

t	m	l	t
b	d	e	b
r	r	n	s
y	q	y	f
g	g	q	l

Directions: Circle the letter that matches the first letter.

Home Activity: Point to each letter and have your child say the letter name.

Name ______________________

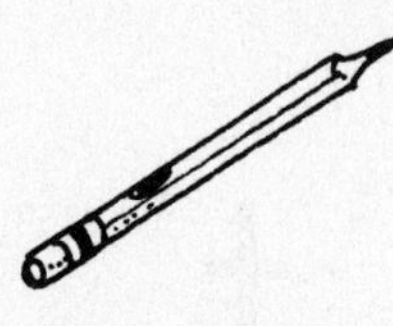

name book pencil

Draw and Write.

Directions: Draw a picture of something in the classroom. Write a label.

Home Activity: Have your child name the letters in *name, book,* and *pencil.*

Name ___________________________

Draw lines.

1.

2.

3.

4.

Directions: Draw lines connecting the pictures whose names rhyme.

Home Activity: Read poems from a children's book and ask your child to listen for rhyming words.

Name ______________________

Draw a line.

1.

2.

3.

4.

Directions: Draw a line to match pictures whose names begin alike.

Home Activity: Point to each picture and have your child name a word that begins like the picture name.

Name ______________________________

Circle.

E	E	F	H	I
P	R	D	P	W
V	W	O	V	S
C	C	L	K	B

Directions: Circle the letter that matches the first letter.

Home Activity: Point to each letter and have your child say the letter name.

Name ____________________________

Circle.

p	g	w	h	p
c	e	c	g	m
v	b	n	v	w
e	p	o	e	c

Directions: Circle the letter that matches the first letter.

Home Activity: Name letters on the page and have your child point to the correct ones.

Name ______________________

Boys

Girls

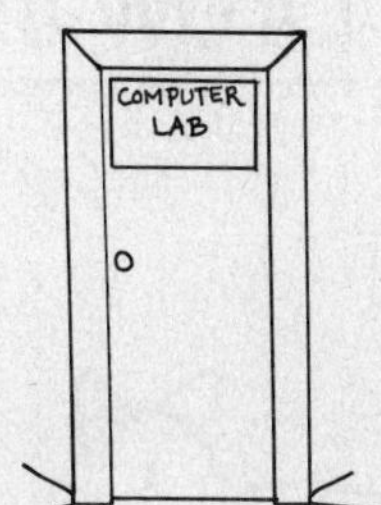

Computer Lab

Draw and Write.

Directions: Draw a sign you see in shcool. Write a label.

Home Activity: Have your child name the letters in the signs.

Name ______________________________

Draw lines.

1.

2.

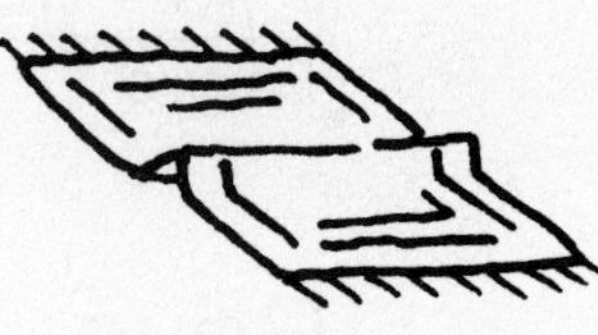

3.

4.

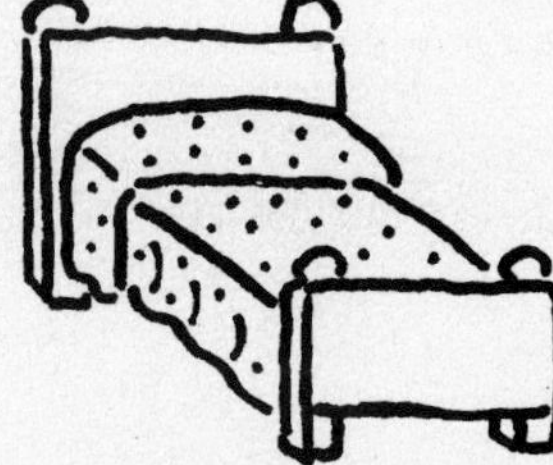

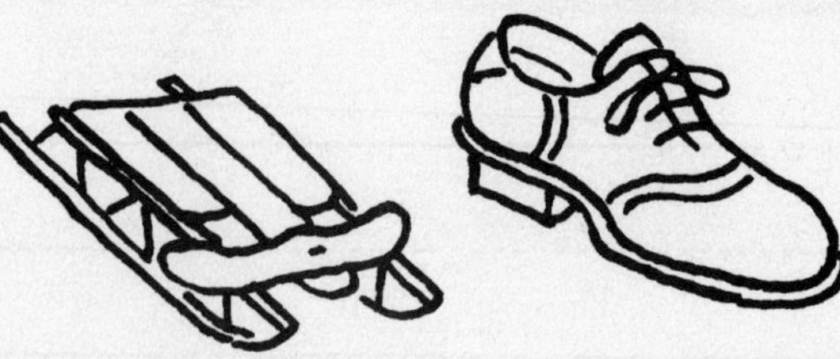

Directions: Draw lines connecting the pictures whose names rhyme.

Home Activity: Encourage your child to make up rhymes—*I see a bug, Living in a rug.*

Name ______________________

Draw lines.

1.

2.

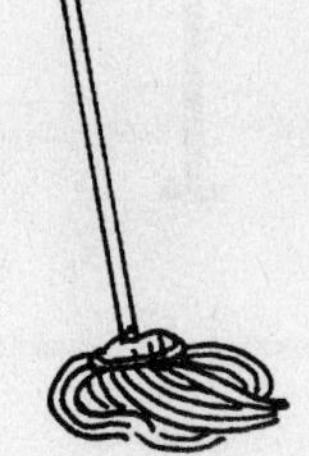

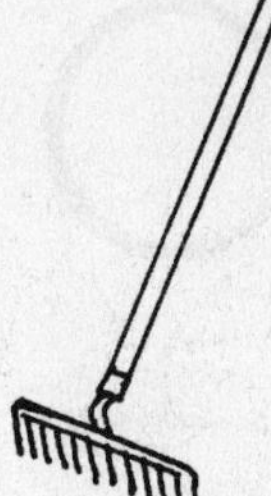

3.

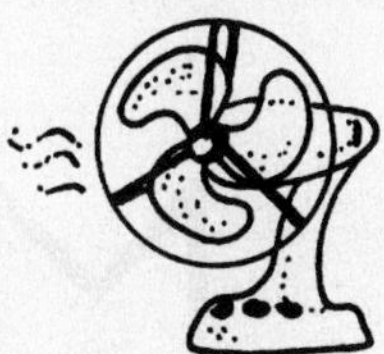

4.

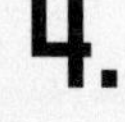

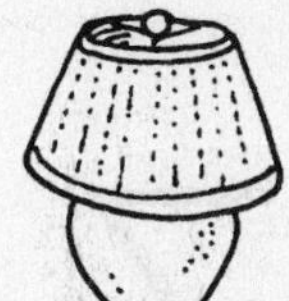
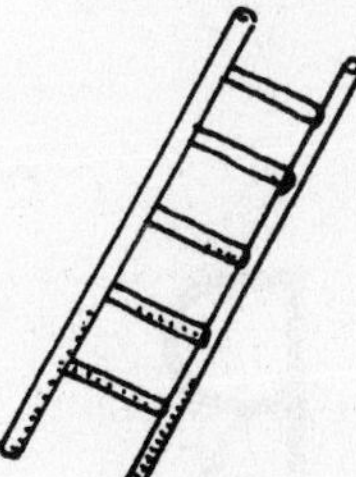

Directions: Draw lines to match the pictures whose names begin alike.

Home Activity: Help your child draw pictures of things whose names begin alike.

Name ______________________

Circle.

I	I	T	P	L
O	K	L	U	O
Q	O	E	R	Q
Z	Z	N	M	K
K	R	S	K	B

Directions: Circle the letter that matches the first letter.

Home Activity: Point to each letter and have your child say the letter name.

Name ______________________________

 Circle.

i	t	i	b	m
z	v	o	p	z
k	l	k	j	h
o	u	p	o	n
q	q	p	g	k

Directions: Circle the letter that matches the first letter.

 **Home Activity:** Point to each letter and have your child say the letter name.

Name ______________________

bus jet house

Draw and Write.

Directions: Draw a picture of something at the grocery store. Write a label.

Home Activity: Have your child name the letters in *bus, jet,* and *house.*

Name ____________________________________

Draw lines.

1.

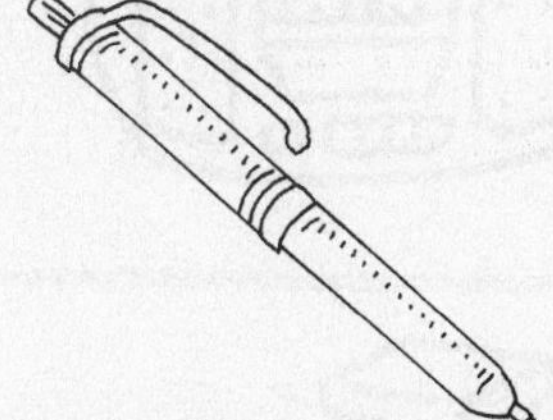

2.

3.

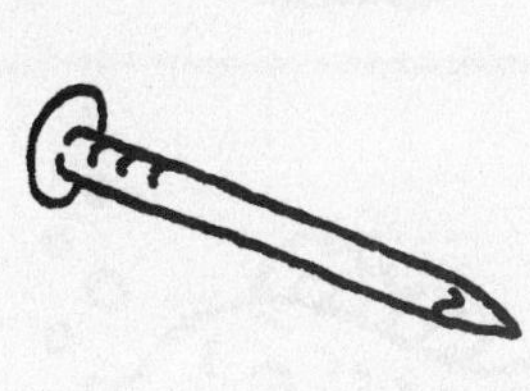

4.

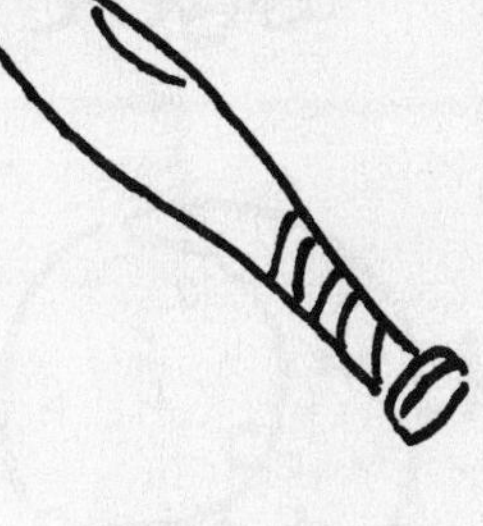

Directions: Draw lines connecting the pictures whose names rhyme.

Home Activity: Read poems from a children's book and ask your child to listen for rhyming words.

Name ______________________________

Circle.

1.    

2.    

3.    

4. 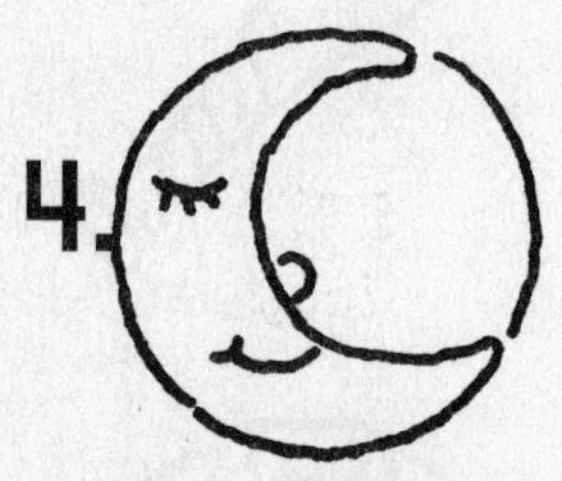   

5.    

Directions: In each row, circle the pictures that begin with the same sound as the first picture.

Home Activity: Say one of the picture names and have your child name a word that begins with the same sound.

Name ______________________________

Circle.

L	F	D	L	I
U	V	U	W	T
X	H	X	B	R
F	R	K	B	F

Directions: Circle the letter that matches the first letter.

Home Activity: Help your child find and name matching letters in newspapers and magazines.

Name ________________________________

Circle.

x	s	t	b	x
u	u	a	d	o
f	k	f	t	j
l	i	y	b	l

Directions: Circle the letter that matches the first letter.

Home Activity: Write a letter from this page and help your child write the same letter.

Name ______________________

A B C D E F G H I J
K L M N O P Q R S T
U V W X Y Z

Write.

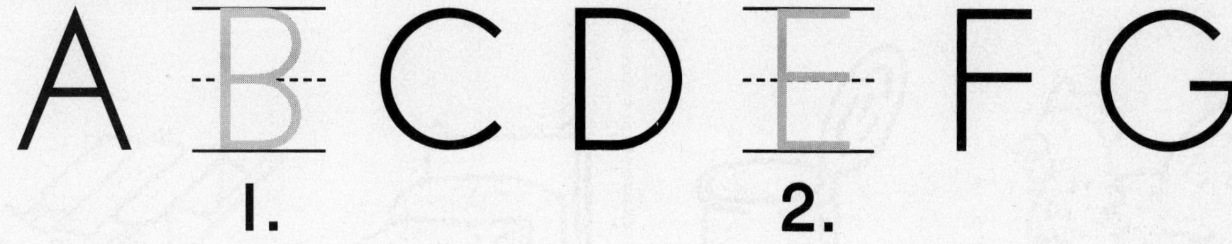

H I J K L M N

3. 4. 5.

O P Q R S T U

6. 7.

V W X Y Z

8. 9. 10.

Directions: Write the missing letters on the lines. Use the alphabet as a guide.

Home Activity: Read the alphabet aloud with your child. Then point to letters and have your child name each letter.

Name ____________________

Draw lines.

1.

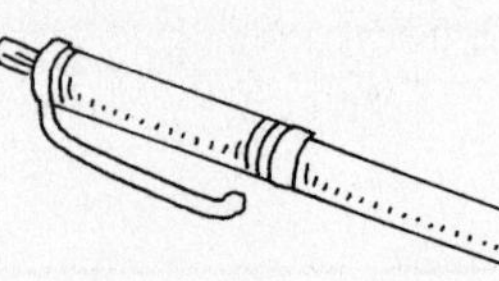

2.

3.

4.

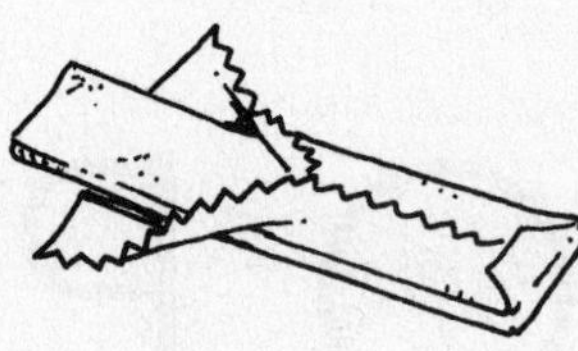

Directions: Draw lines connecting the pictures whose names rhyme.

Home Activity: Ask your child to listen for rhyming words as you read a book of rhymes aloud.

Name ____________________

Circle.

1.  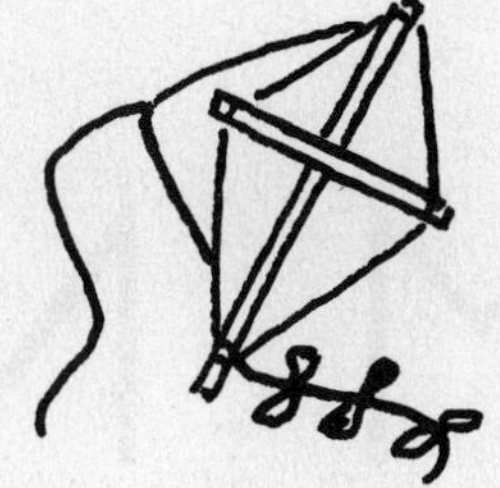 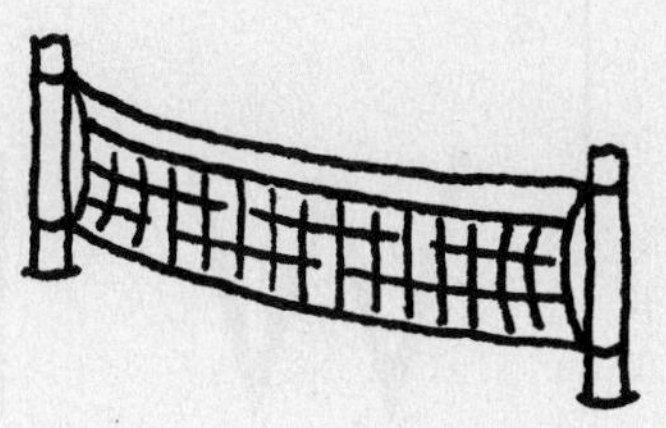 

2.    

3.    

4.    

5.    

Directions: In each row, circle the pictures that begin with the same sound as the first picture.

Home Activity: Give a clue to an animal and have your child name the animal and the beginning sound—*I have a shell.* (*turtle*, *t*)

Name ____________________

Circle.

W	W	M	N	H
N	Y	K	M	N
H	F	H	P	U
S	S	C	O	J

Directions: Circle the letter that matches the first letter.

Home Activity: Point to each letter and have your child say the letter names.

Name ______________________________

Circle.

n	u	m	n	r
h	n	h	b	g
s	c	s	f	x
w	m	n	v	w

Directions: Circle the letter that matches the first letter.

Home Activity: Help your child find these letters around the house.

Name ______________________________

a b c d e f g h i j
k l m n o p q r s t
u v w x y z

Write.

a b __c__ d e __f__ g
1. 2.

h __i__ j k l __m__ n
3. 4.

o p __q__ r __s__ t u
5. 6.

__v__ w x y __z__
7. 8.

Directions: Write the missing letters on the lines. Use the alphabet as a guide.

Home Activity: Read the alphabet aloud with your child. Then point to letters and have your child name each letter.

Name ______________________________

Circle.

Mm

Directions: Circle the pictures whose names begin like *mouse*.

Home Activity: Ask your child to think of other words that begin like *mouse*.

Name ______________________

Circle.

1\. Mm

2\. Mm

3\. Mm

4\. Mm

Directions: In each box, circle the pictures whose names begin with *m*.

Home Activity: As you say different words, ask your child to identify those that begin with *m*.

Name ______________________________

Color.

1. m

2. m

 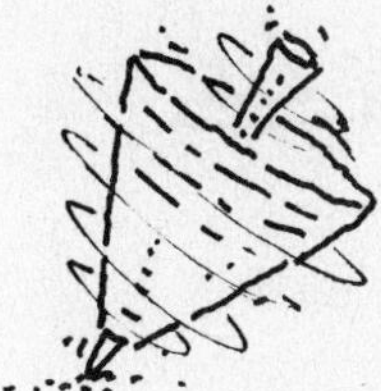 

3. m

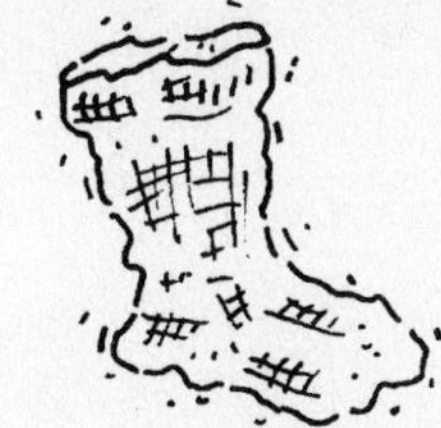  

4. m

5. m

Directions: In each row, color the picture that begins like *mouse*.

Home Activity: Help your child make up two-word phrases with words that begin with *m*—*moody mouse* or *many monkeys*.

Name ______________________

Draw lines.

Directions: Draw lines from the letters to the pictures that begin with that sound.

Home Activity: As you say different words, ask your child to identify those that begin with *m*.

Name ___________________________

Draw lines.

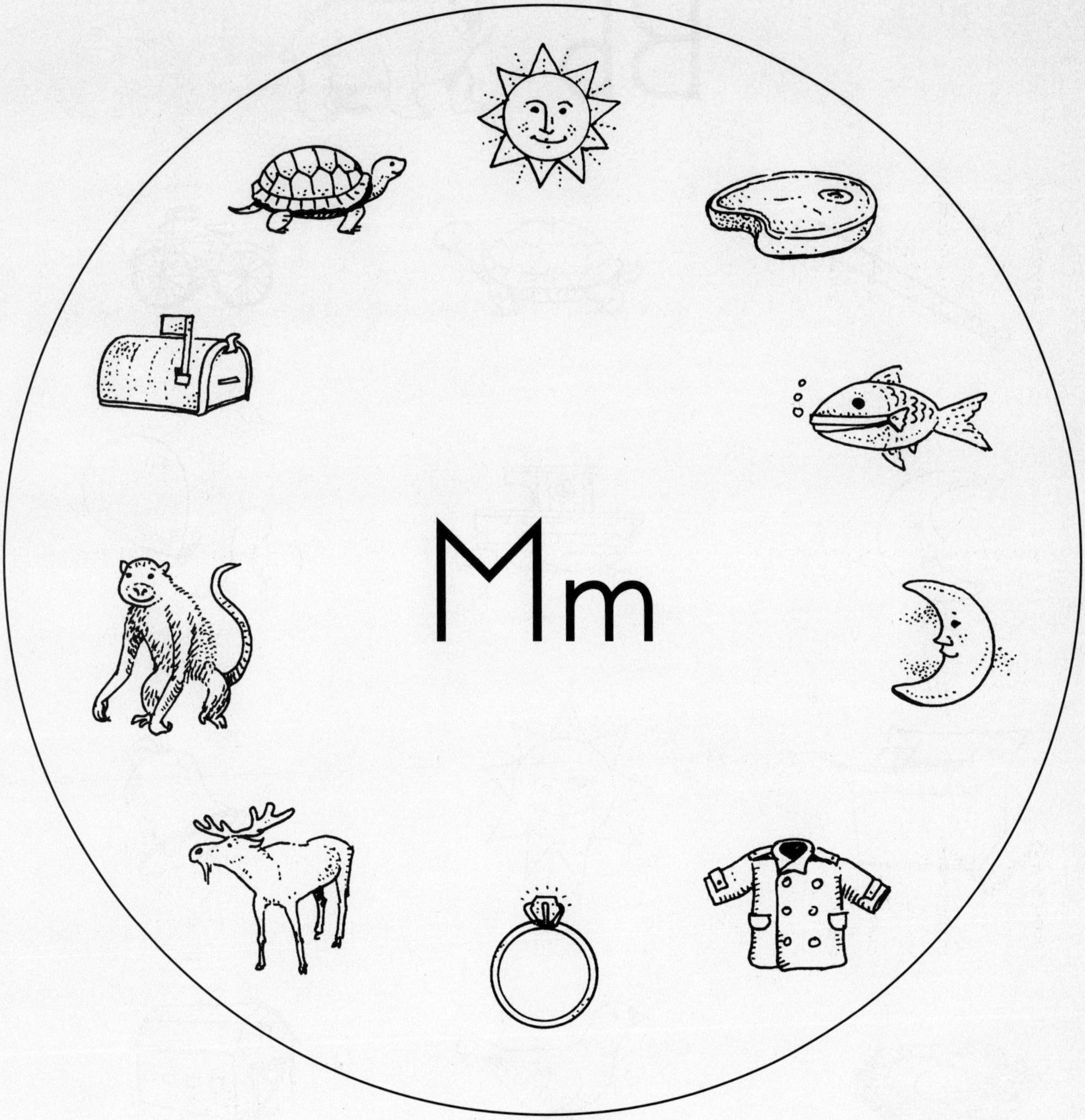

Mm

Directions: Draw lines connecting the letters in the middle with the pictures on the circle that begin with *m*.

Home Activity: Ask your child to identify animals whose names begin with *m*.

Name ____________________

Circle.

Bb

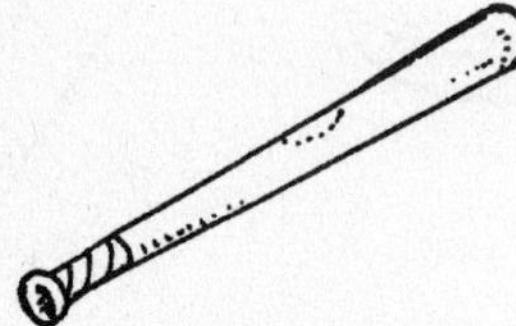

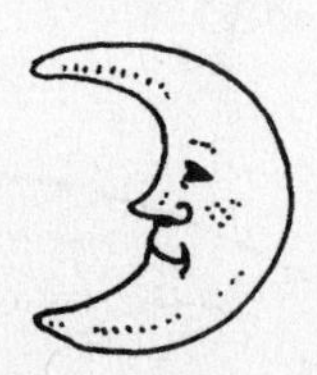

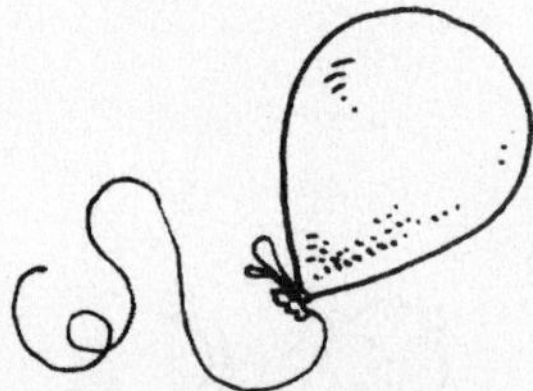

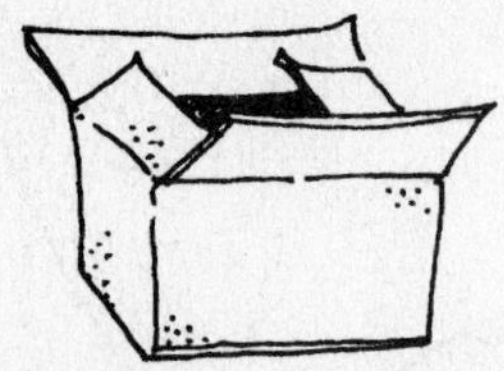

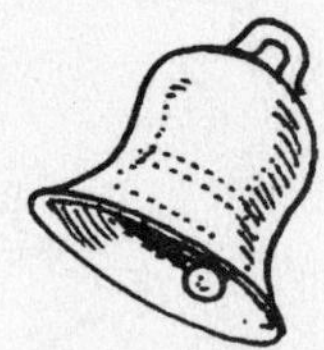

Directions: Circle the pictures whose names begin like *bear*.

Home Activity: Ask your child to make rhyming words that begin with *b* for these words: *tell* (*bell*), *cat* (*bat*), *fox* (*box*).

Name ______________________

Circle.

1. Bb

2. Bb

3. Bb

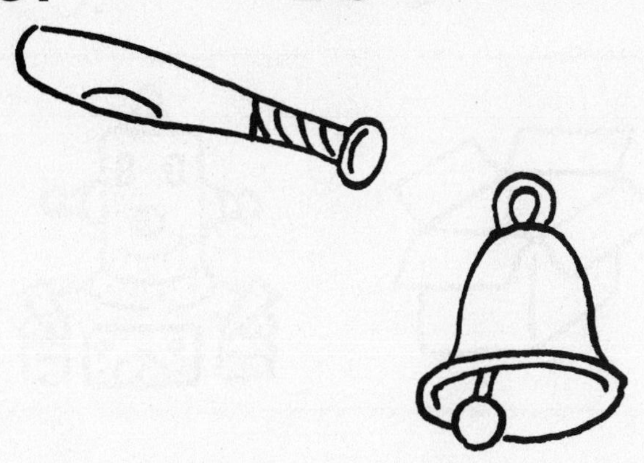

4. Bb

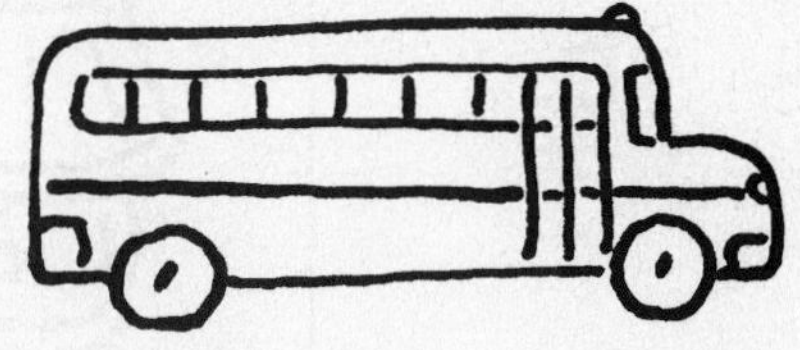

Directions: In each box, circle the pictures whose names begin with *b*.

Home Activity: As you say different words, ask your child to identify those that begin with *b*.

Name ______________________________

Color.

1. b

2. b

3. b

 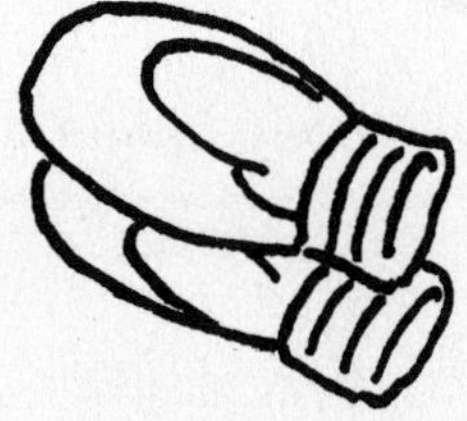 

4. b

5. b

Directions: In each row, color the picture that begins like *bear*.

Home Activity: Help your child make up tongue twisters with *b* words—*Busy Bobby Bee bakes berry bagels.*

Name ______________________________

Draw lines.

Bb

Bb

Directions: Draw lines from the letters to the pictures that begin with that sound.

Home Activity: Play "I'm going to Buffalo and I'll take ____," repeating the sentence and adding words that begin with *b*.

Name ______________________________

Draw lines.

Bb

Directions: Draw lines connecting the letters in the middle with the pictures on the circle that begin with *b*.

Home Activity: Make up riddles for the *b* pictures and ask your child to find the answers—*It bounces.* (*ball*) *It floats.* (*boat*)

Name ______________________________

Circle.

Ss 

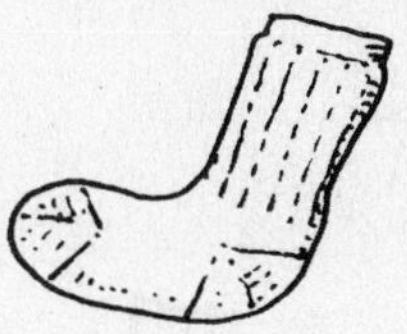

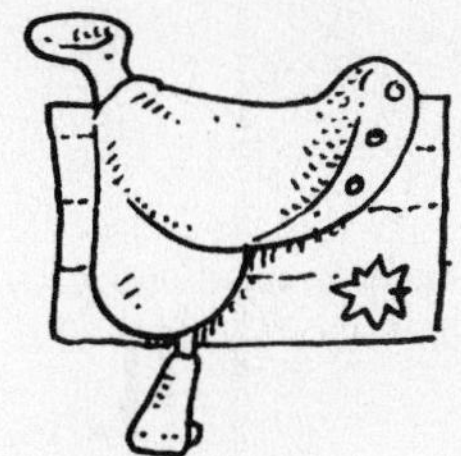

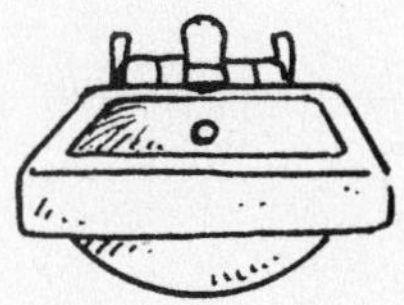

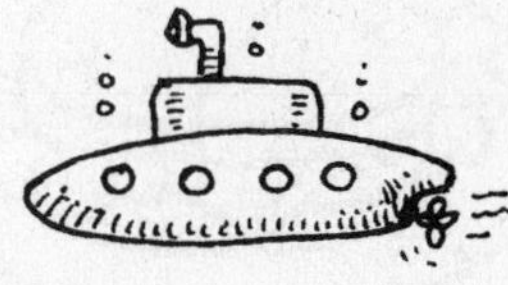

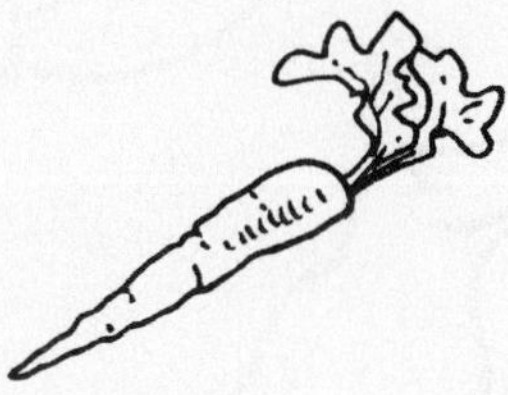

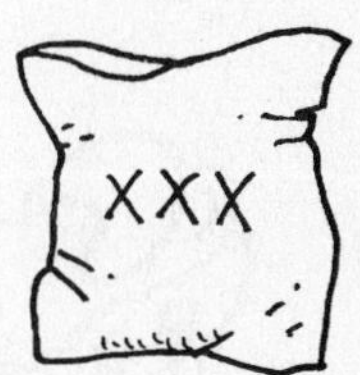

Directions: Circle the pictures whose names begin like *sun*.

Home Activity: Have your child draw a sun and write the letter *s* on it.

Name ______________________

Circle.

1\. Ss

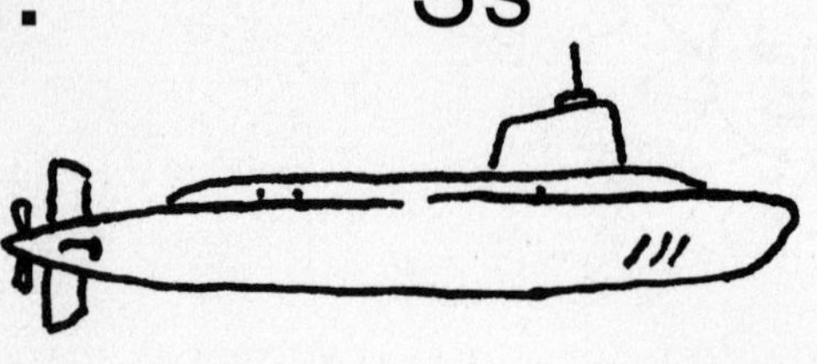

2\. Ss

3\. Ss

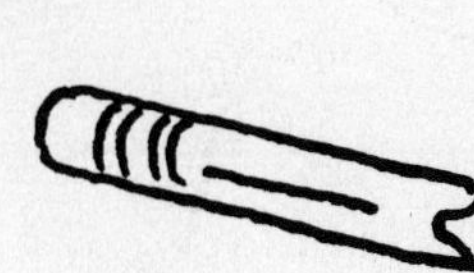

4\. Ss

Directions: In each box, circle the pictures whose names begin with *s*.

Home Activity: Write the letter *s* on a sheet of paper. Have your child draw things that begin with the letter *s*.

Name ______________________________

Color.

1. s 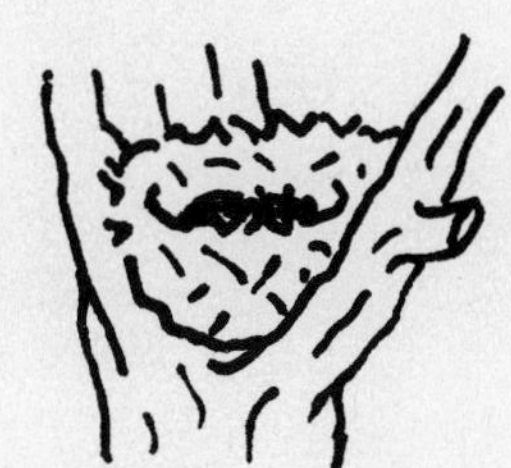  

2. s   

3. s   

4. s   

5. s  

Directions: In each row, color the picture whose name begins like *sun*.

Home Activity: Help your child make up two-word phrases with words that begin with *s—silly snake* or *sunny seal*.

Name ______________________________

Draw lines.

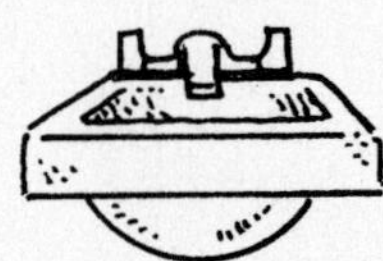

Ss

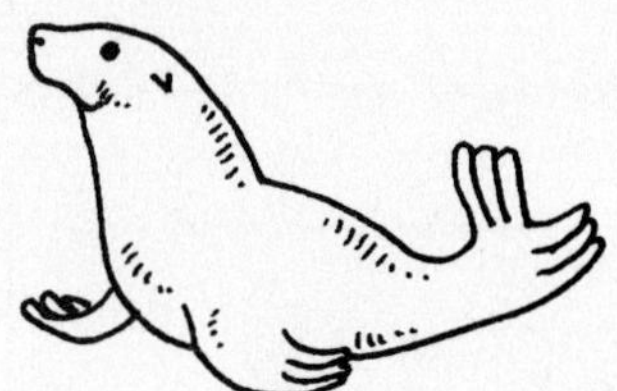

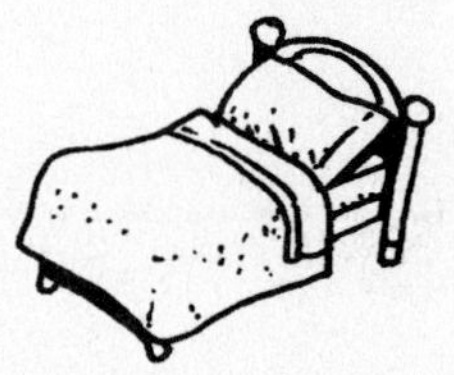

Ss

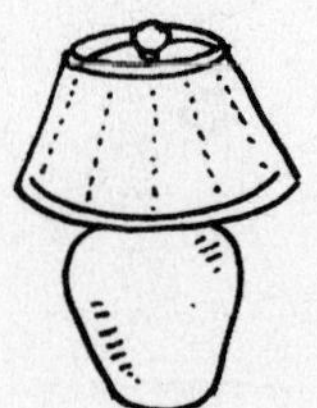

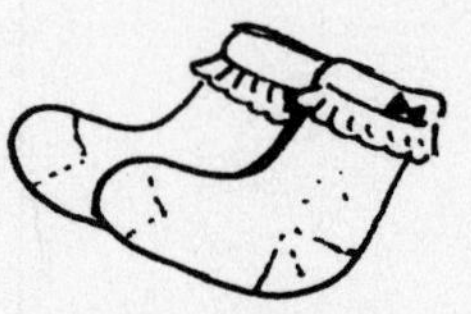

Directions: Draw lines from the letters to the pictures that begin with that sound.

Home Activity: Have your child draw pictures of things that begin with *s* on a sack.

Name ______________________________

Draw lines.

Ss

Directions: Draw lines connecting the letters in the middle with the pictures on the circle that begin with *s*.

Home Activity: Have your child name foods that begin with *s*.

Name ____________________

Circle.

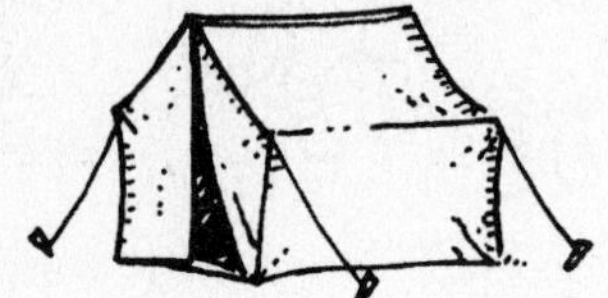

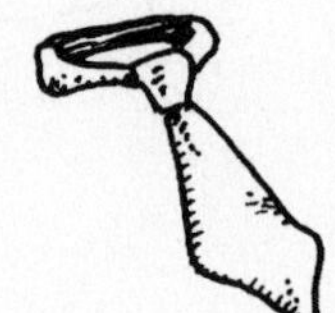

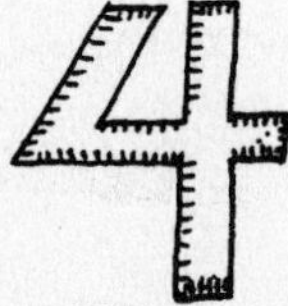

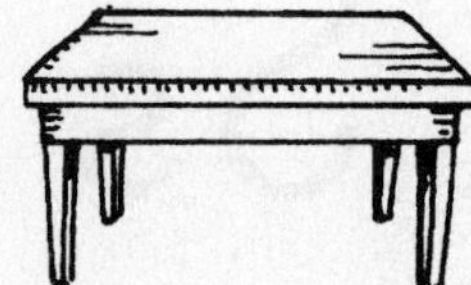

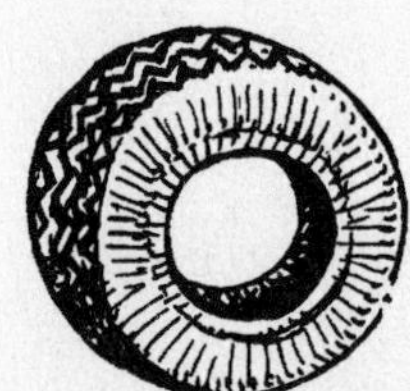

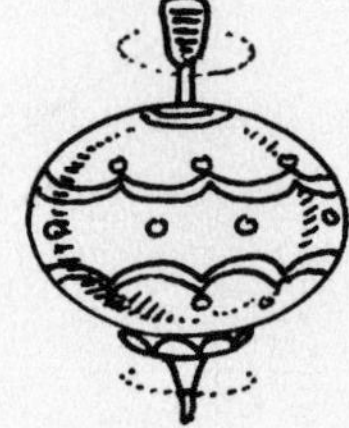

Directions: Circle the pictures whose names begin like *tiger*.

Home Activity: Ask your child to name other words that begin like *tiger*.

Name ______________________________

Circle.

1. Tt

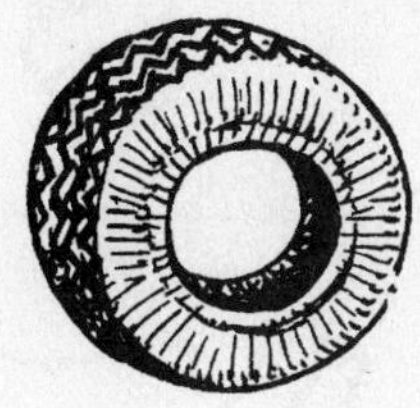

2. Tt

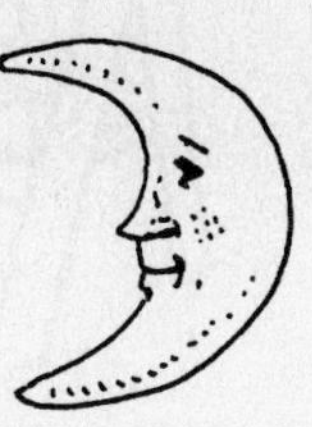

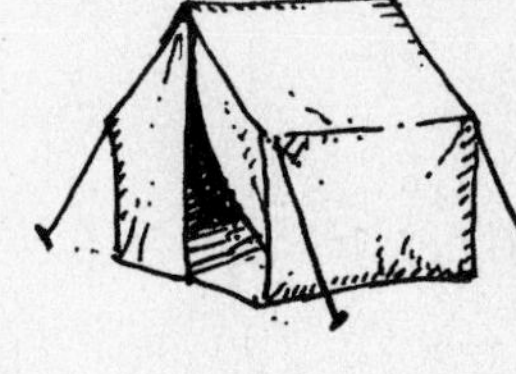

3. Tt

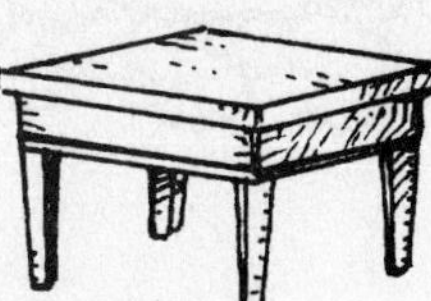

4. Tt

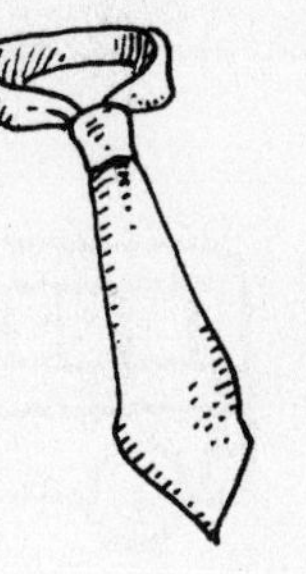

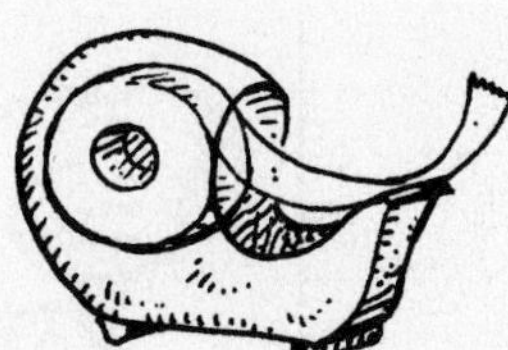

Directions: In each box, circle the pictures whose names begin with *t*.

Home Activity: As you say different words, ask your child to identify those that begin with *t*.

Name ______________________

Color.

1. t

2. t

3. t

 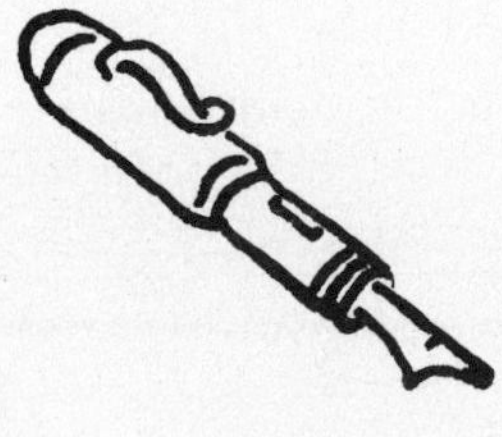 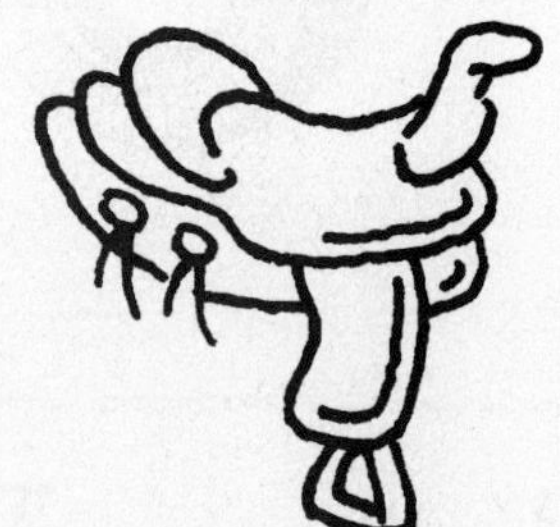

4. t

5. t

Directions: In each row, color the picture that begins like *tiger*.

Home Activity: Help your child make up two-word phrases with words that begin with *t*—*talking turkey* or *tall tale*.

Name ______________________

Draw lines.

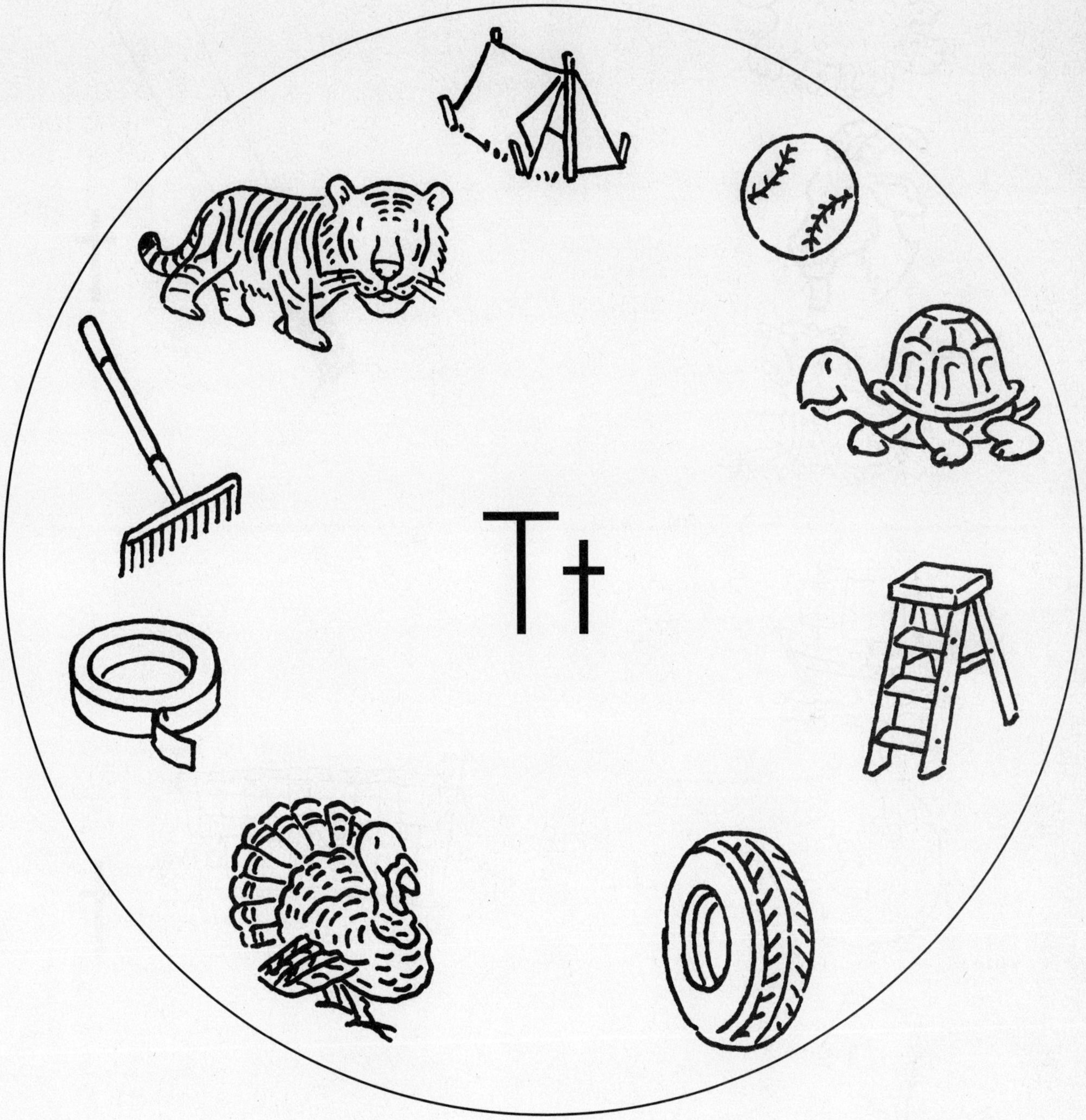

Tt

Directions: Draw lines connecting the letters in the middle with the pictures on the circle that begin with *t*.

Home Activity: Ask your child to identify animals whose names begin with *t*.

Name ______________________

Draw lines.

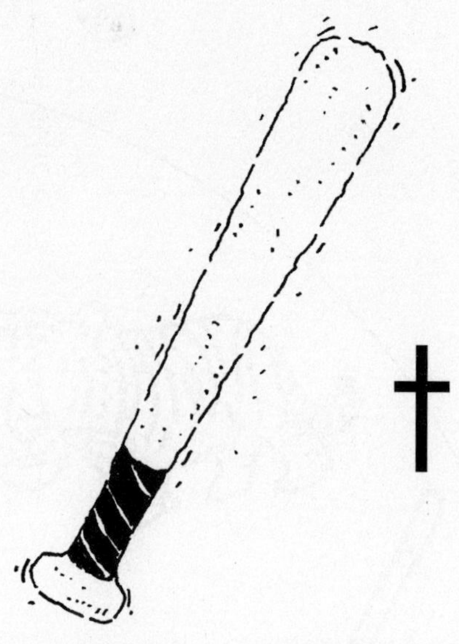

t

t

Directions: Draw lines to match the pictures whose names end with /t/.

Home Activity: Make a card with the letter *t*. Ask your child to hold up the card each time you say a word that ends with *t*.

Name ___________________________________

Circle.

Ff

Directions: Circle the pictures whose names begin like *fox*.

Home Activity: Say two words and have your child tell which word begins like *fox*.

Name ______________________________

Circle.

1. Ff

2. Ff

3. Ff

4. Ff

Directions: In each box, circle the pictures whose names begin with *f*.

Home Activity: Point to and name a picture on the page. Have your child wiggle one finger if the word begins like *finger*.

Name ______________________________

Color.

1.	f			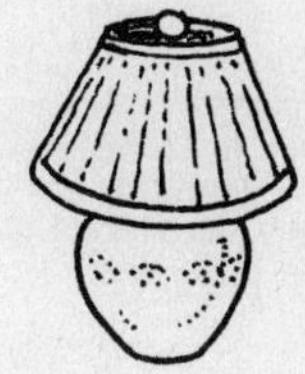
2.	f		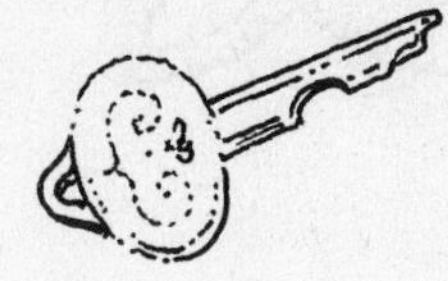	
3.	f		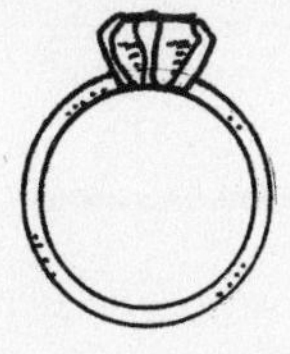	
4.	f			
5.	f			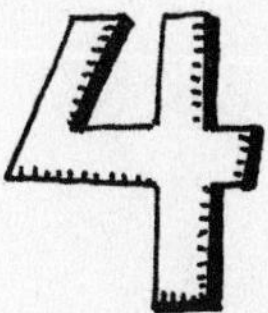

Directions: In each row, color the picture that begins like *fox*.

Home Activity: Draw a fish on a large sheet of paper and have your child draw pictures of other things that begin like *fish*.

Name ______________________________ Consonant *f*

Draw lines.

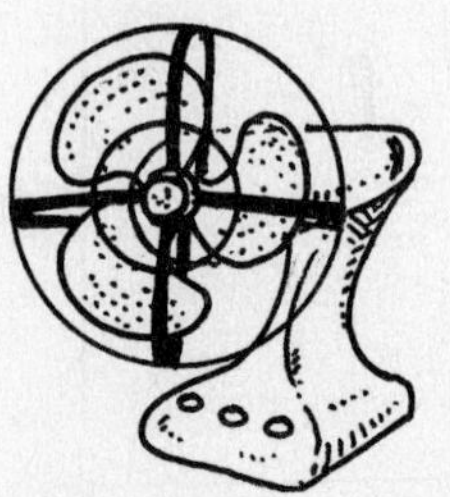

Directions: Draw lines from the letters to the pictures that begin with that sound.

Home Activity: As you say different words, ask your child to identify those that begin with *f*.

Name ______________________________

Draw lines.

5

Ff

Directions: Draw lines connecting the letters in the middle with the pictures on the circle that begin with *f*.

Home Activity: Say the word *feet* and have your child point to them. Continue with *face, finger, foot.*

Name ______________________________

Color.

cat

Directions: Color the pictures whose names have the short *a* sound.

Home Activity: Have your child name other words with the short *a* sound.

Name ______________________

Draw a line.

1.

2.

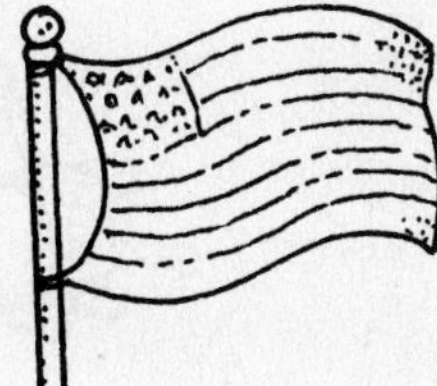

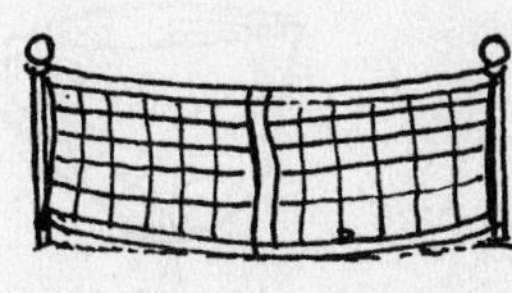

3.

4.

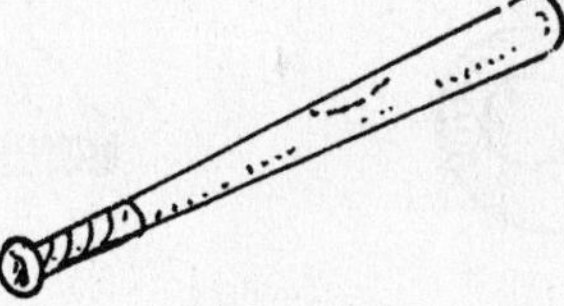

Directions: Draw a line to match the pictures with the short *a* sound.

Home Activity: Have your child name words that rhyme with *cat—bat, fat, hat, mat, pat, rat, sat.*

Name ______________________________

Circle.

1.

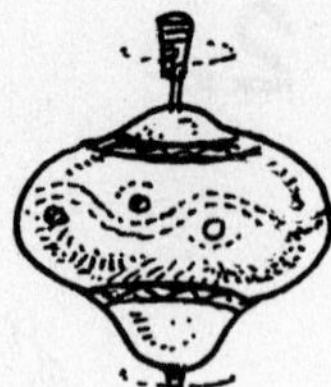

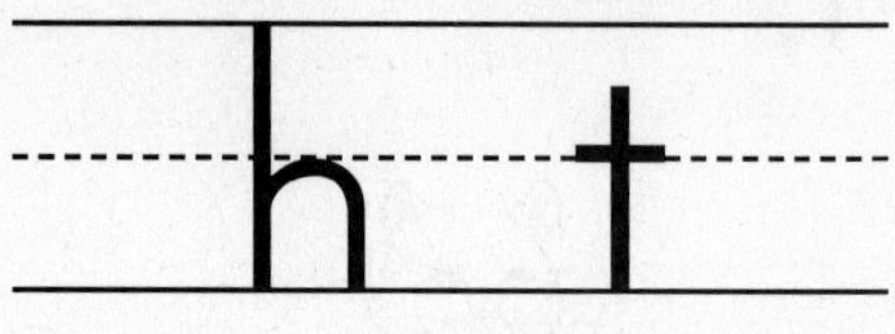

2.

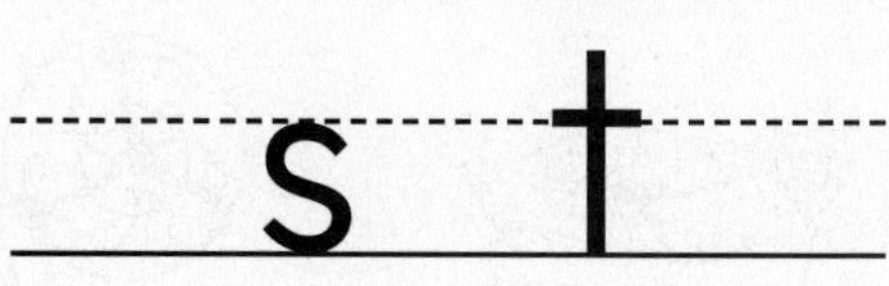

3.

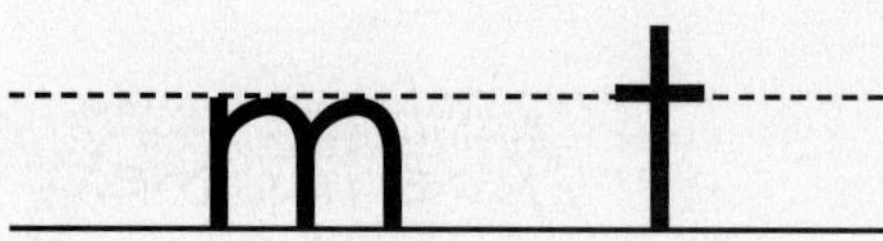

4.

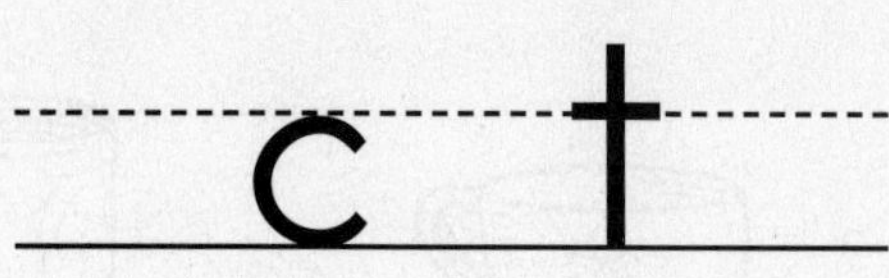

Directions: In each row, circle the picture with the short *a* sound. Write the letter to finish the picture name.

Home Activity: Make letter cards for *c*, *t*, *h*, *s*, *m*, and *a*. Help your child arrange the letters to make the words on this page.

Name ______________________________

Color.

1. 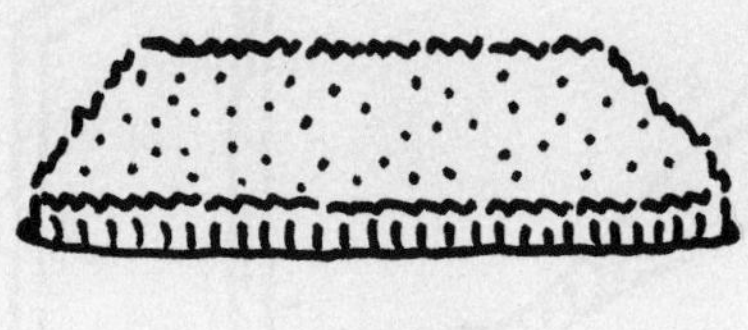

mat

2. 

fat

3. 

sat

4. 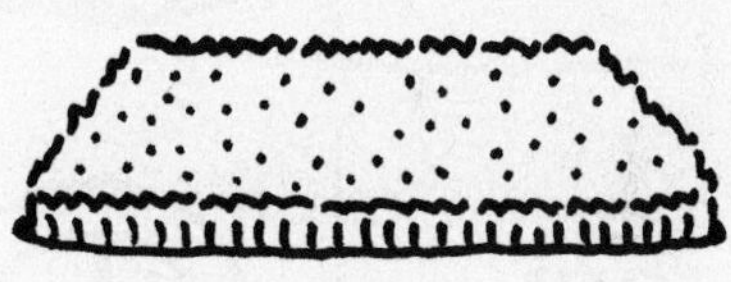

mat

Directions: In each box, color the picture that rhymes with the word at the top of the box.

Home Activity: Write the word *can* on a sheet of paper. Help your child write words that rhyme with *can*.

Name ______________________

Circle.

1. bat

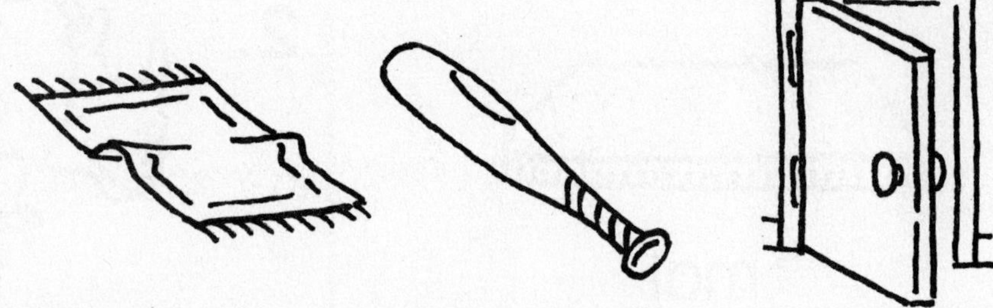

2. rat

3. cat

4. mat

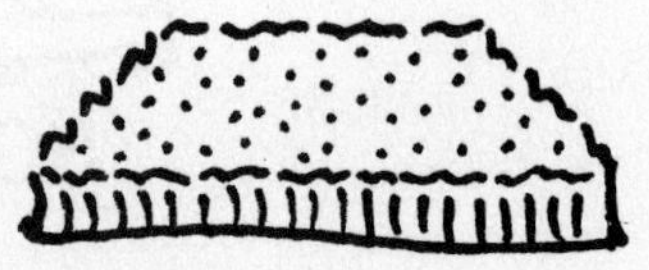

5. hat

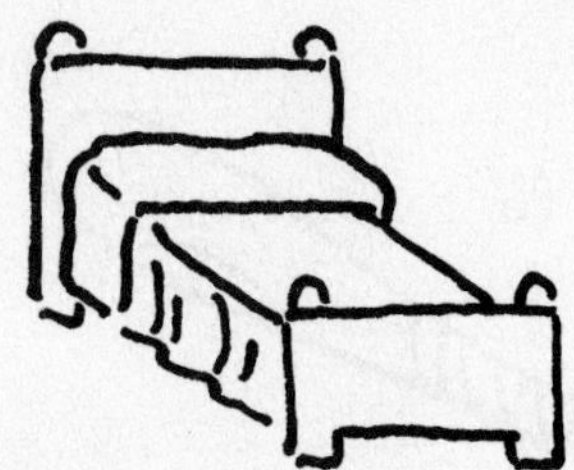

Directions: In each row, circle the picture the word names.

Home Activity: Point to a word on the page and have your child use the word in a sentence.

Name ______________________________

Circle.

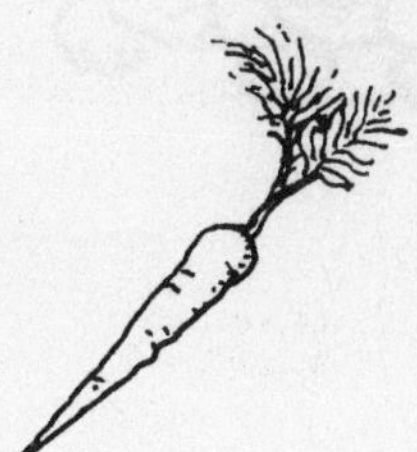

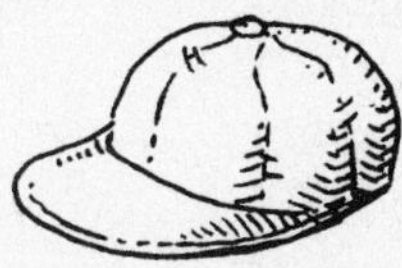

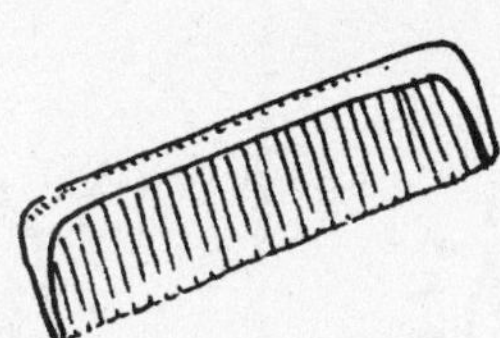
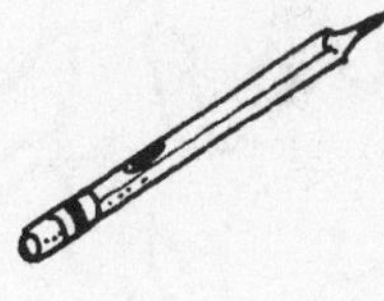

Directions: Circle the pictures whose names begin like *cat*.

Home Activity: Draw a cat. Have your child say a word that begins with *c* and write a *c* on the cat.

Name ____________________

Circle.

1. Cc

2. Cc

3. Cc

4. Cc

Directions: In each box, circle the pictures whose names begin with *c*.

Home Activity: Say two words from the page and ask your child to tell if the words begin with *c*.

Name ______________________

Color.

1. c  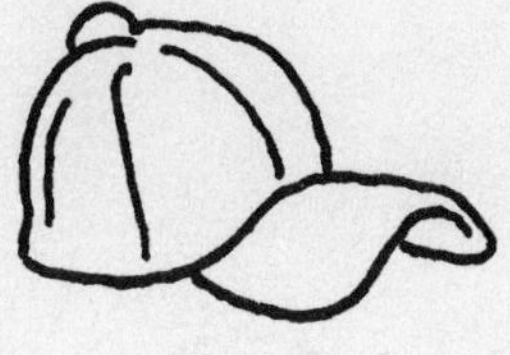 

2. c 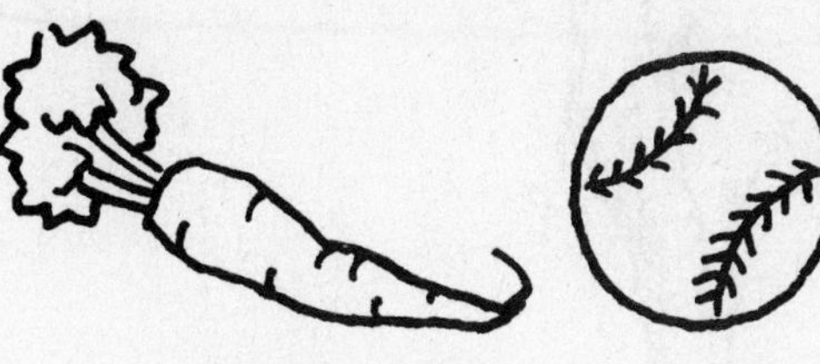 

3. c   

4. c   

5. c 

Directions: In each row, color the picture that begins like *cat*.

Home Activity: Help your child draw pictures of things that begin with *c*.

Name ______________________

Draw lines.

Cc

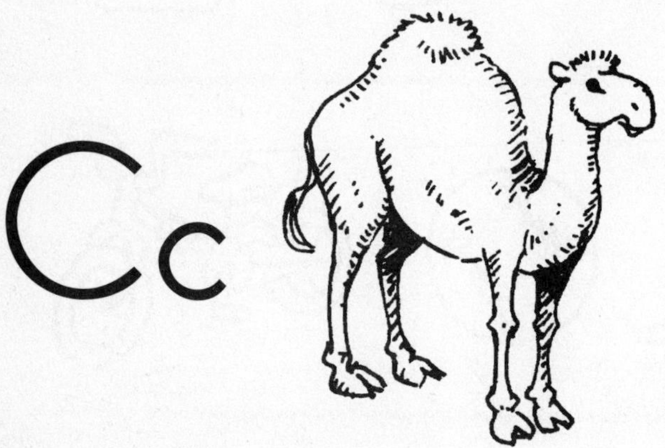

Cc

Directions: Draw lines from the letters to the pictures that begin with that sound.

Home Activity: Write many letter *c*'s. Have your child name a word that begins with *c* and circle one of the *c*'s.

Name ______________________________

Draw lines.

Cc

Directions: Draw lines connecting the letters in the middle with the pictures on the circle that begin with *c*.

Home Activity: Ask your child to name foods that begin with *c*. *(cake, corn, carrots, cookies, cucumbers)*

Name ______________________

Circle.

Pp

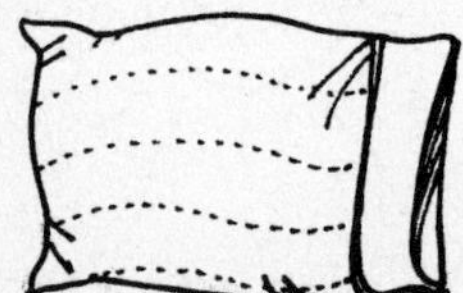

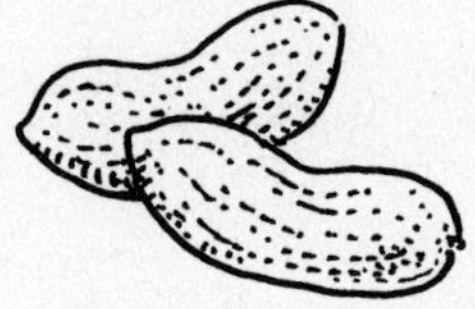

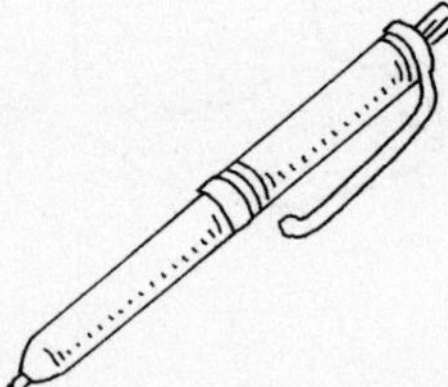

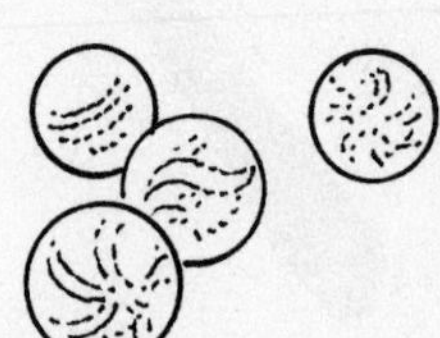

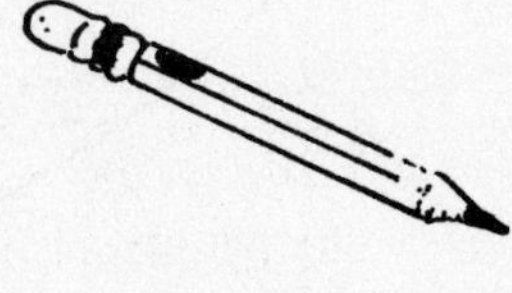

Directions: Circle the pictures whose names begin like *pig*.

Home Activity: Ask your child to name foods that begin with *p*. (*peanuts, pineapple, pears, peaches, pancakes*)

Name ______________________

Circle.

1. Pp

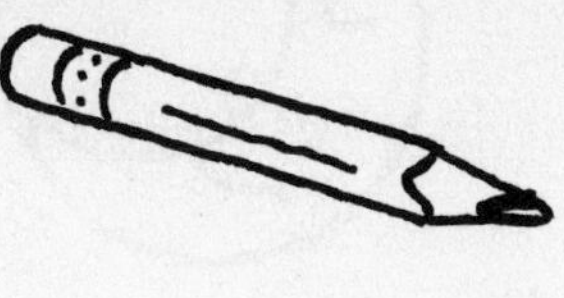

2. Pp

3. Pp

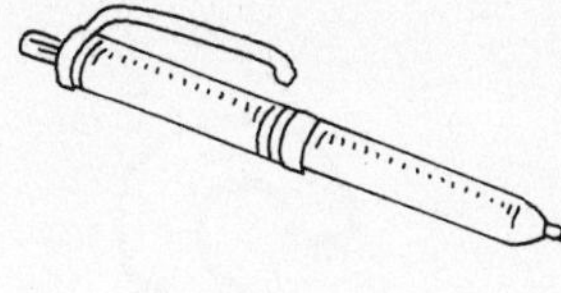

4. Pp

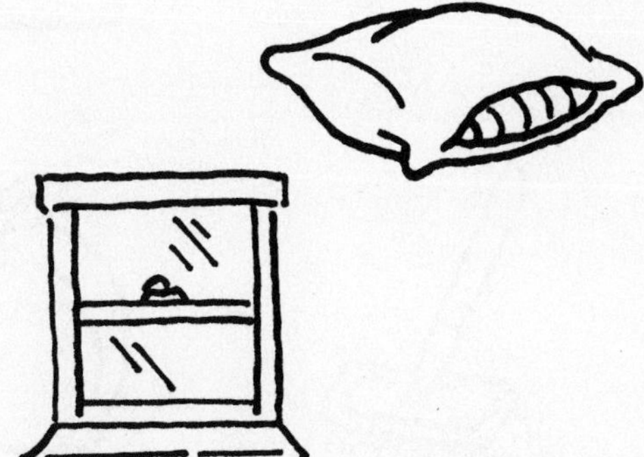

Directions: In each box, circle the pictures whose names begin with *p*.

Home Activity: Give a clue about a word that begins with *p* and ask your child to guess the word—*It says oink!* (*pig*)

Name ______________________________

Color.

1. p

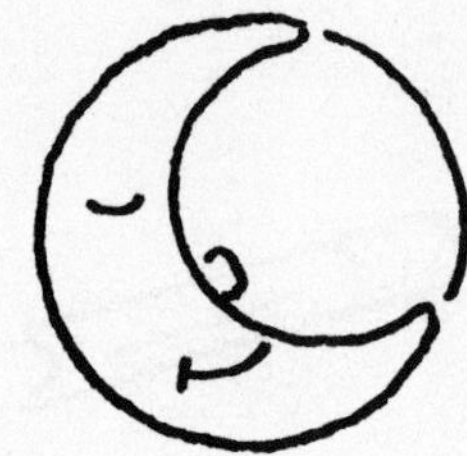

2. p

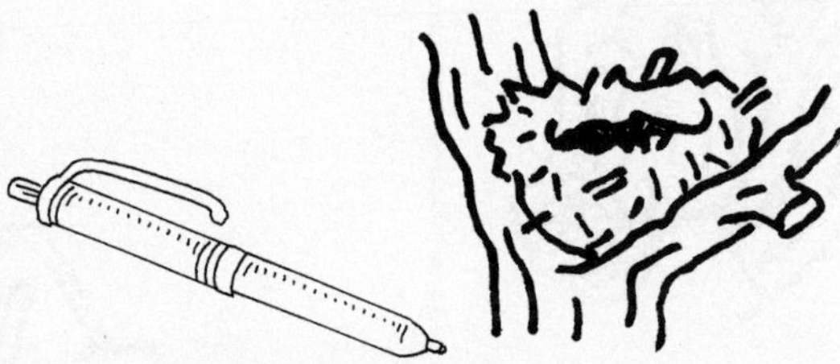

3. p

4. p

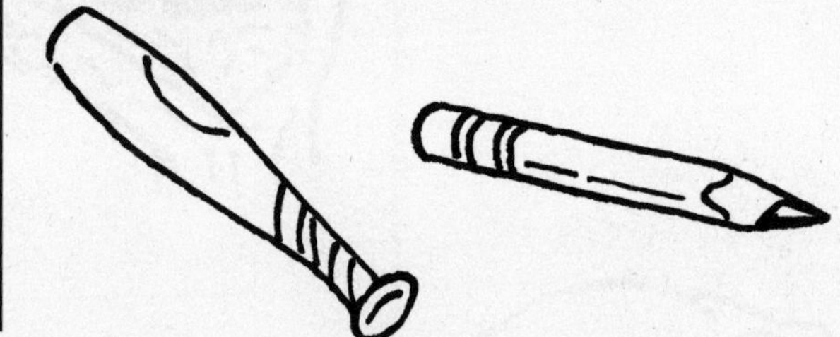

5. p

Directions: In each row, color the picture that begins like *pig*.

Home Activity: Help your child write words (or draw pictures) that begin with *p*.

Name ______________________________

Draw lines.

Pp

Directions: Draw lines connecting the letters in the middle with the pictures on the circle that begin with *p*.

Home Activity: Hold up a penny and ask your child to name words that begin with the same sound as *penny*.

Name ____________________

Draw lines.

p

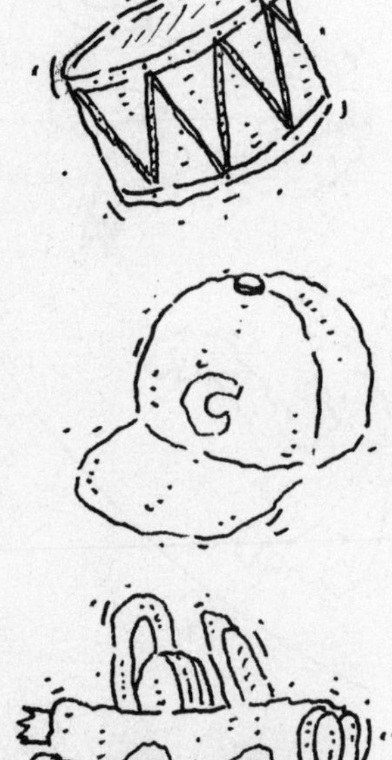

p

Directions: Draw lines to match the pictures whose names end with the letter *p*.

Home Activity: Make a card with the letter *p*. Ask your child to hold up the card each time you say a word that ends with *p*.

Name ______________________________

Circle.

Nn

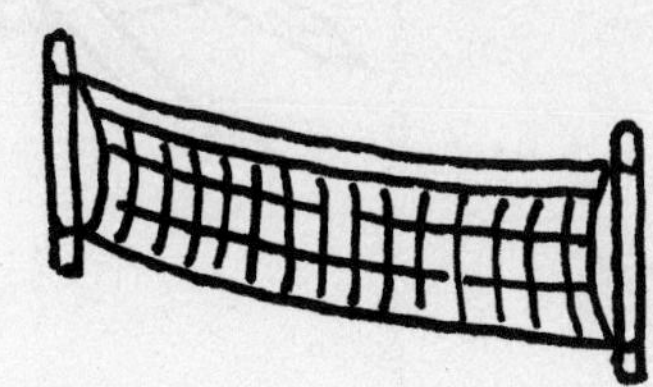

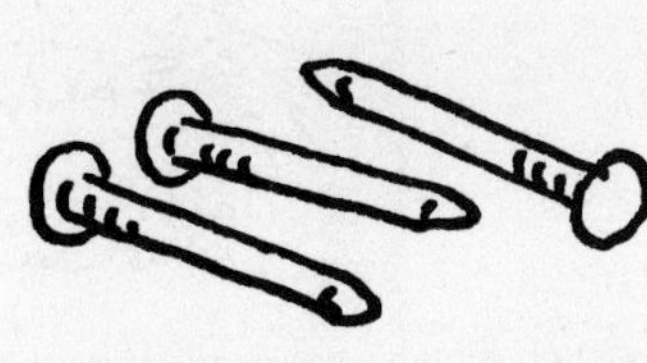

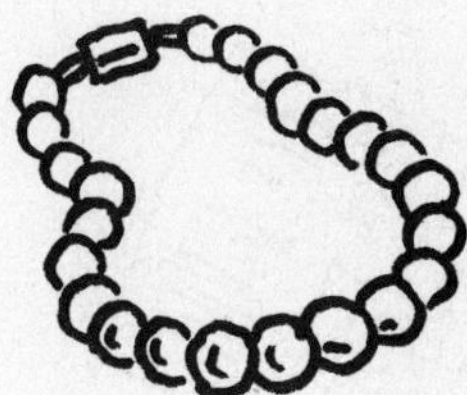

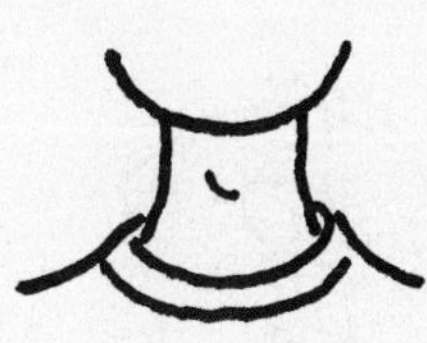

Directions: Circle the pictures whose names begin like *nest*.

Home Activity: Ask your child to think of other words that begin with *n*.

Name ______________________

Circle.

1. Nn

2. Nn

3. Nn

4. Nn

Directions: In each box, circle the pictures whose names begin with *n*.

Home Activity: As you say different words, ask your child to point to his or her nose if the word begins with *n*.

Name ______________________________

Color.

1. n

2. n

3. n

4. n

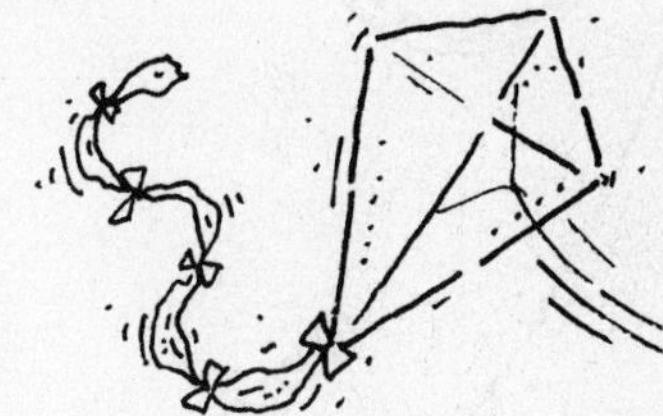

5. n

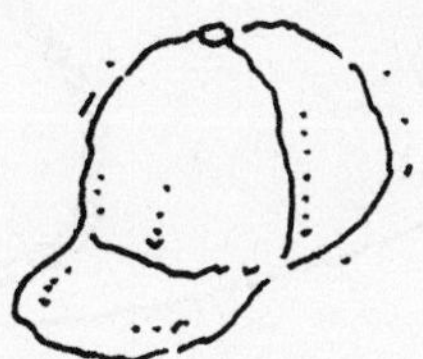

Directions: In each row, color the picture that begins like *nest*.

Home Activity: Help your child draw a nest, write the letter *n*, and write some words in the nest that begin with *n*.

Name ______________________

Draw lines.

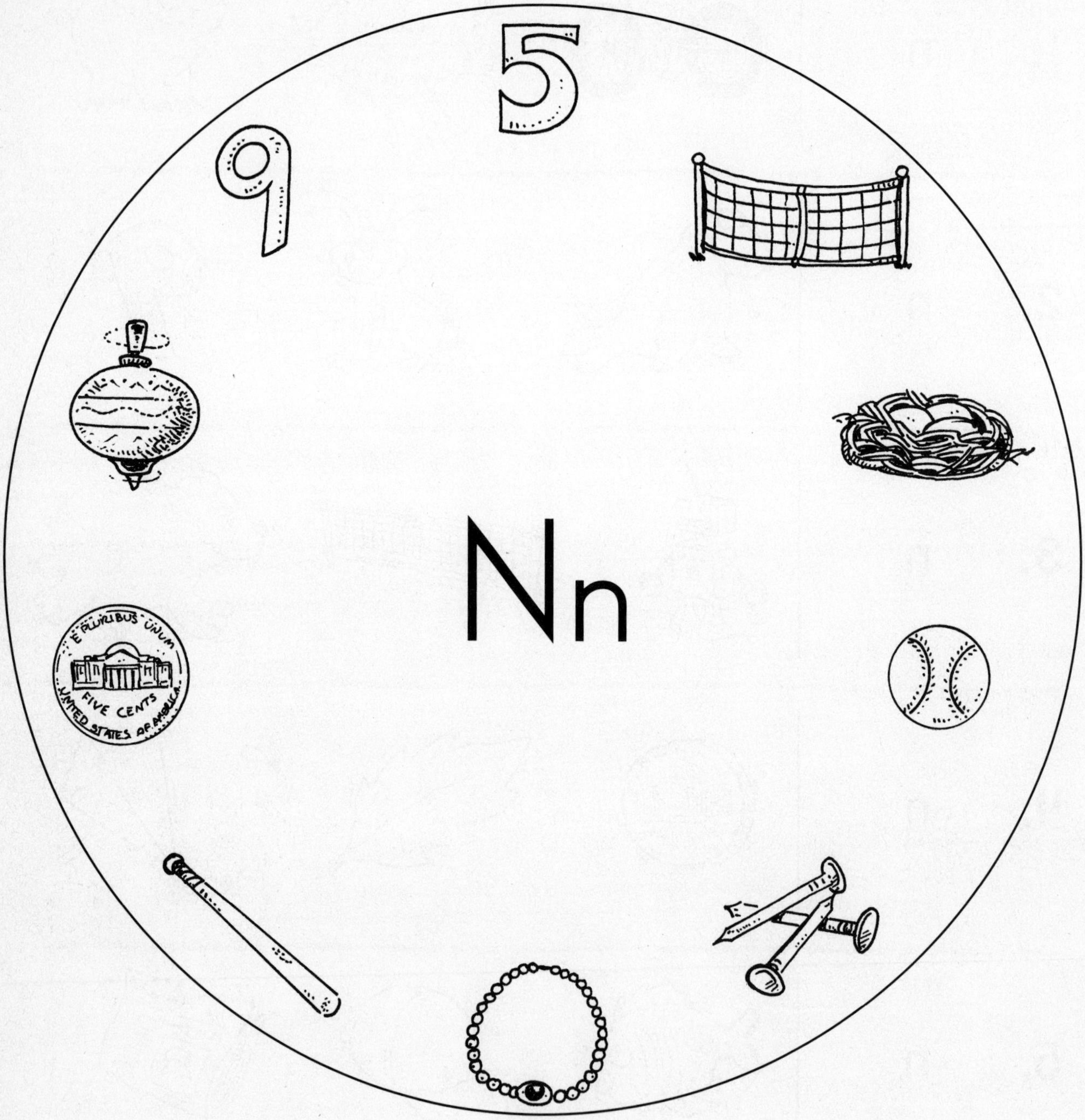

Nn

Directions: Draw lines connecting the letters in the middle with the pictures on the circle that begin with *n*.

Home Activity: Hold up a nickel and have your child name other words that begin like *nickel*.

Name ______________________________

Draw lines.

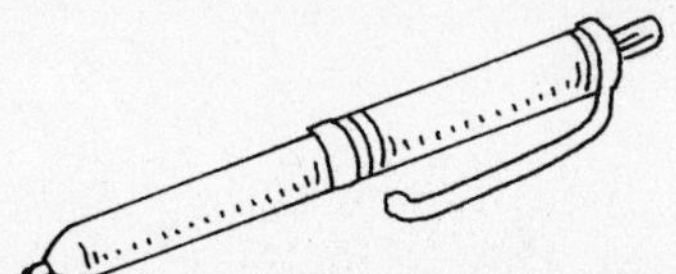

n

n

Directions: Draw lines to match the pictures whose names end with the letter *n*.

Home Activity: Make a card with the letter *n*. Ask your child to hold up the card each time you say a word that ends with *n*.

Name ___________________________

Color.

pig

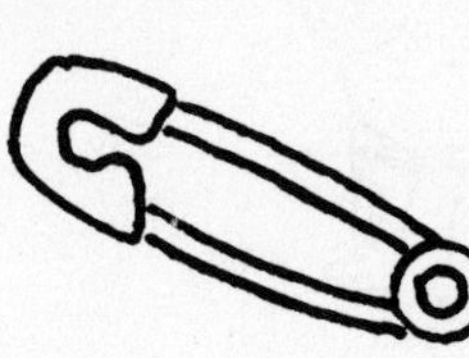

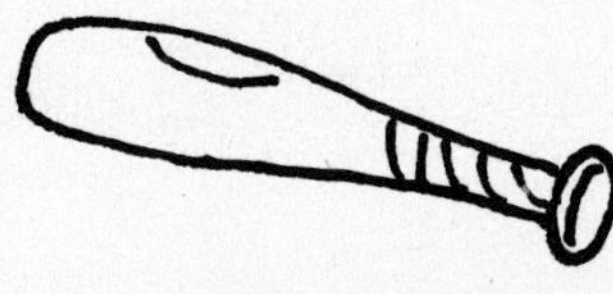

Directions: Color the pictures whose names have the short *i* sound.

Home Activity: Have your child name other words with the short *i* sound.

Name ____________________

Draw a line.

1\.

2\.

3\.

4\.

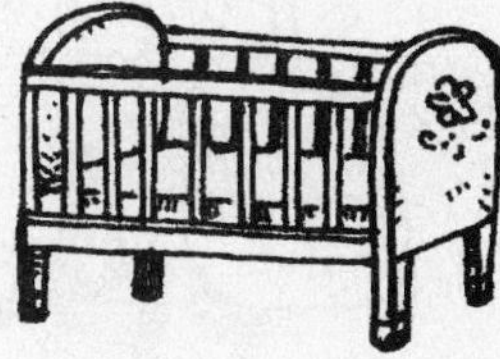

Directions: Draw a line to match the pictures with the short *i* sound.

Home Activity: Have your child name words that rhyme with *pig*—*wig, fig, dig, jig.*

Name ______________________

Circle.

1.

2.

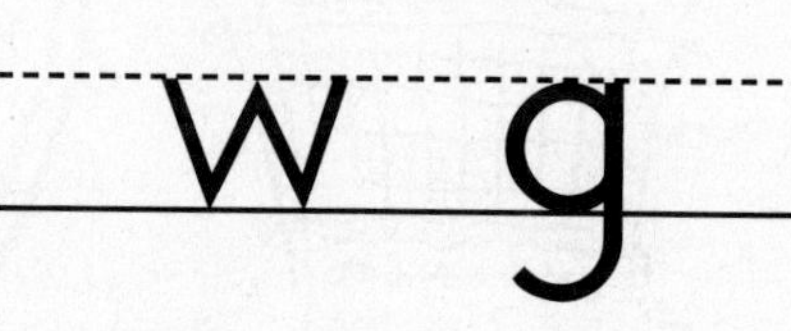

3.

s t

4.

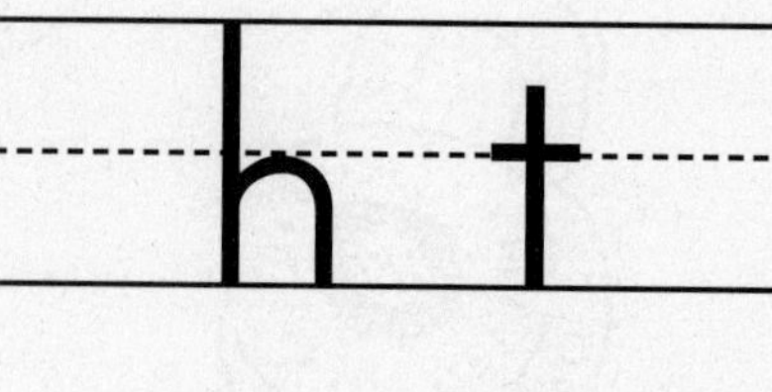

Directions: In each row, circle the picture with the short *i* sound. Write the letter to finish the picture name.

Home Activity: Make letter cards for *p, g, w, s, t, h,* and *i.* Help your child arrange the letters to make the words on this page.

Name ______________________________

Color.

1.

sit

2.

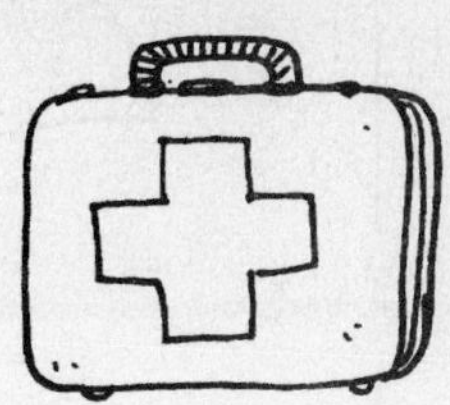

kit

3.

dig

4.

big

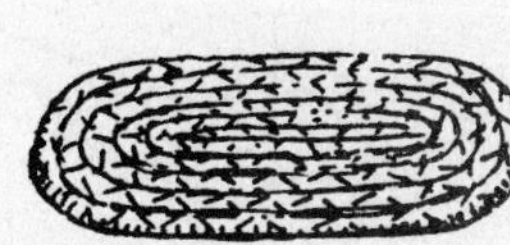

Directions: In each box, color the picture that rhymes with the word at the top of the box.

Home Activity: Write the word *big* on a sheet of paper. Help your child write words that rhyme with *big*.

Name ______________________________

Circle.

1. hit

2. sit

3. bit

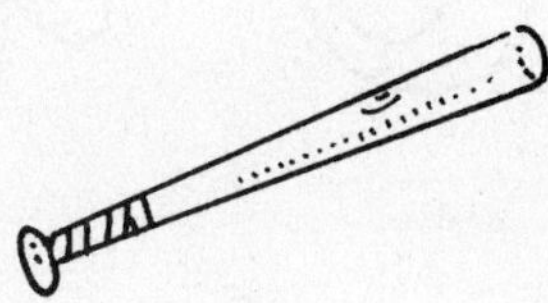

4. fit

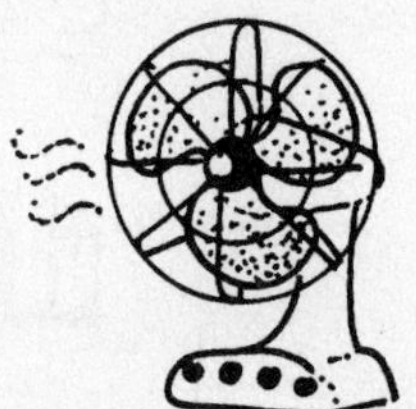

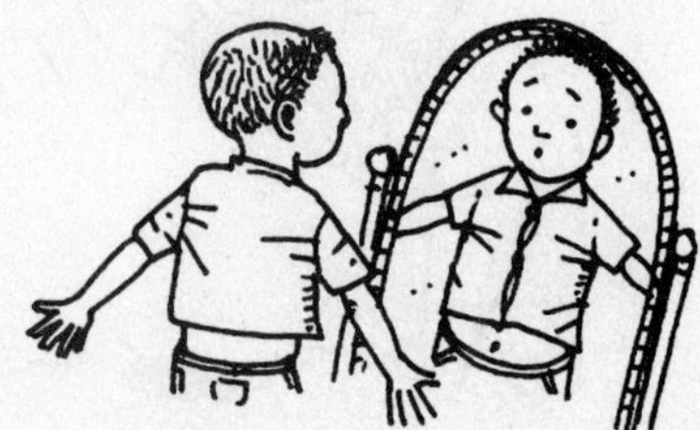

5. kit

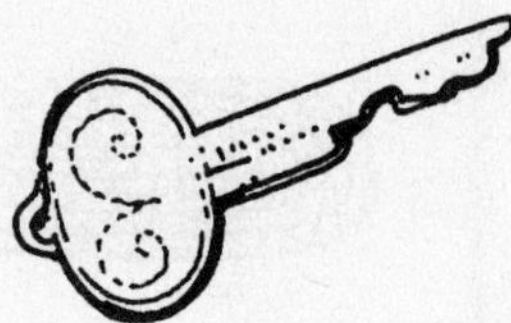

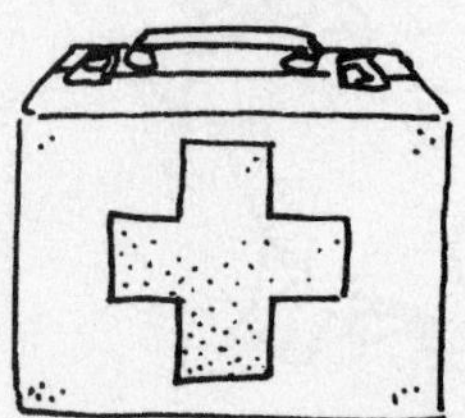

Directions: In each row, circle the picture the word names.

Home Activity: Point to a word on the page and have your child use the word in a sentence.

Name ______________________________

Circle.

Hh

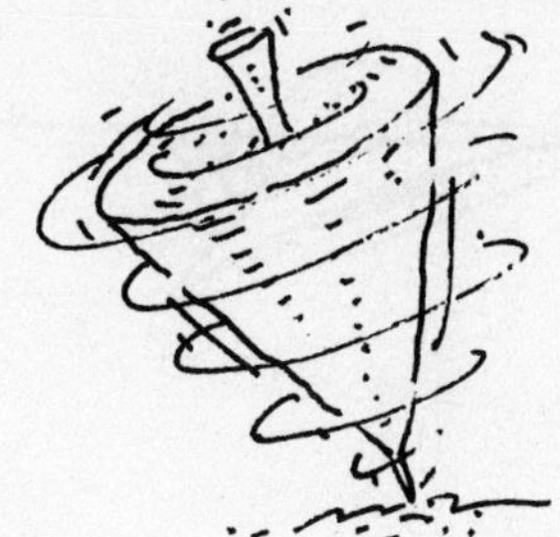

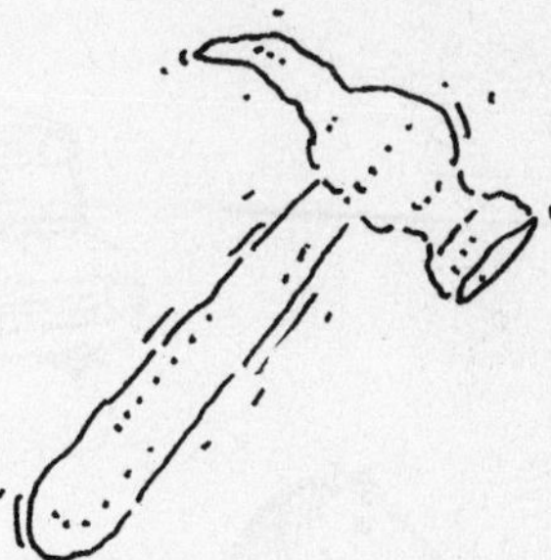

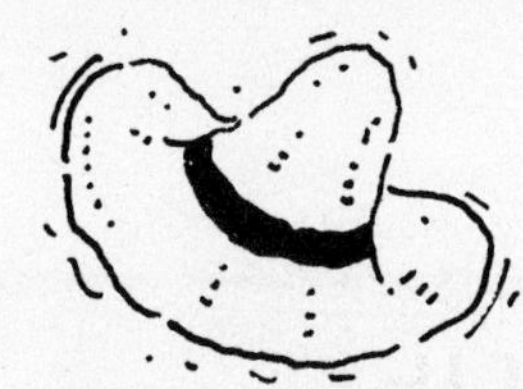

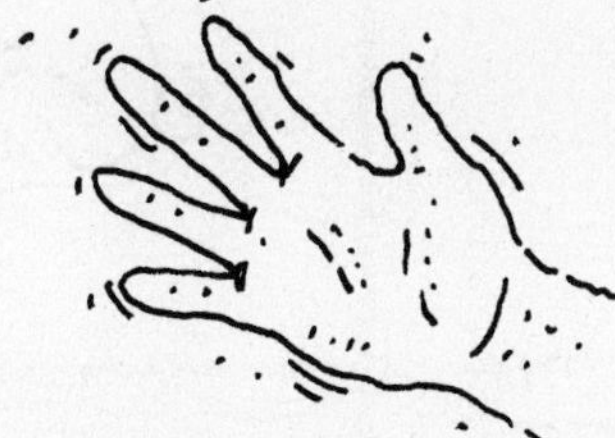

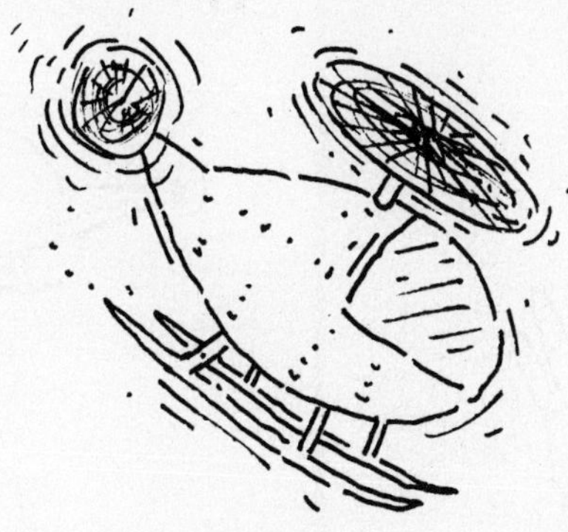

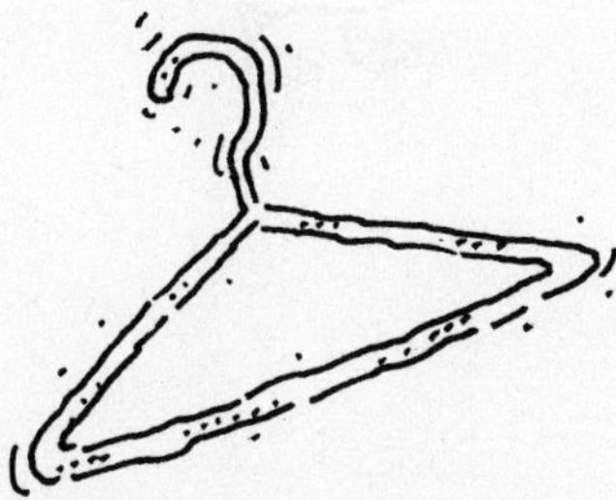

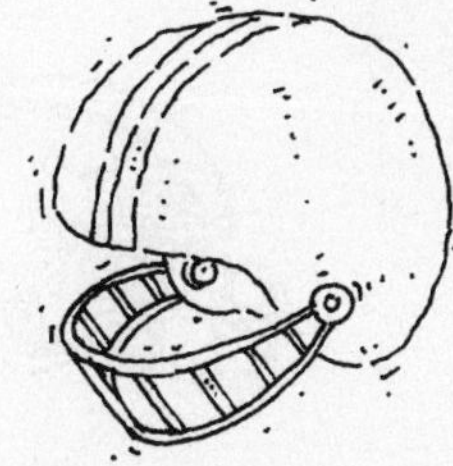

Directions: Circle the pictures whose names begin like *horse*.

Home Activity: Draw a house and ask your child to write words that begin with *h* on the house.

Name ______________________________

Circle.

1. Hh

2. Hh

3. Hh

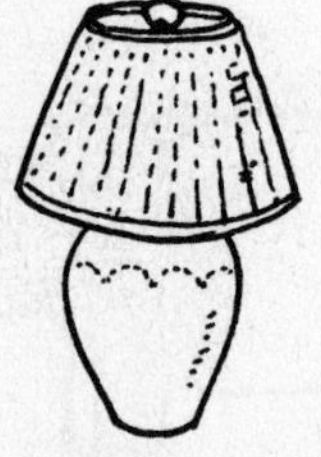

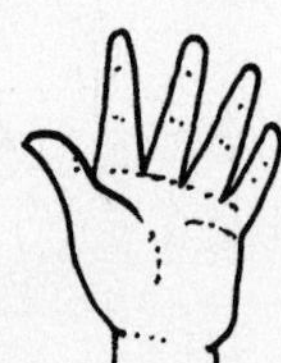

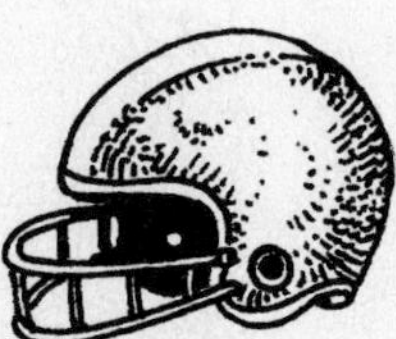

4. Hh

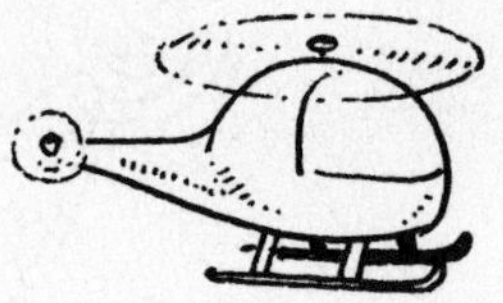

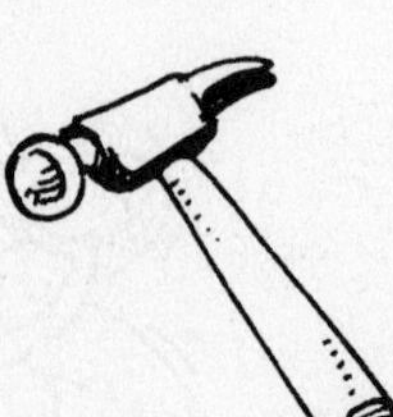

Directions: In each box, circle the pictures whose names begin with *h*.

Home Activity: As you say different words, ask your child to wave his or her hand when you say a word that begins with *h*.

Name ______________________

Color.

1. h 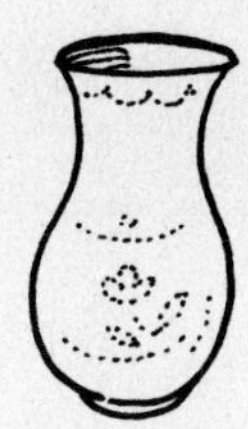  

2. h   

3. h   

4. h  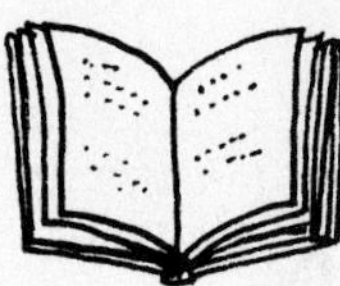 

5. h 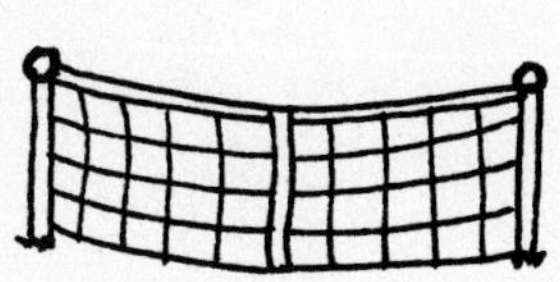  

Directions: In each row, color the picture that begins like *horse*.

Home Activity: Help your child collect objects that begin with *h* and name each item.

Name ______________________

Draw lines.

Directions: Draw lines from the letters to the pictures that begin with that sound.

Home Activity: Have your child put a hat on each time you point to a picture on the page that begins with *h*.

Name ______________________________

Draw lines.

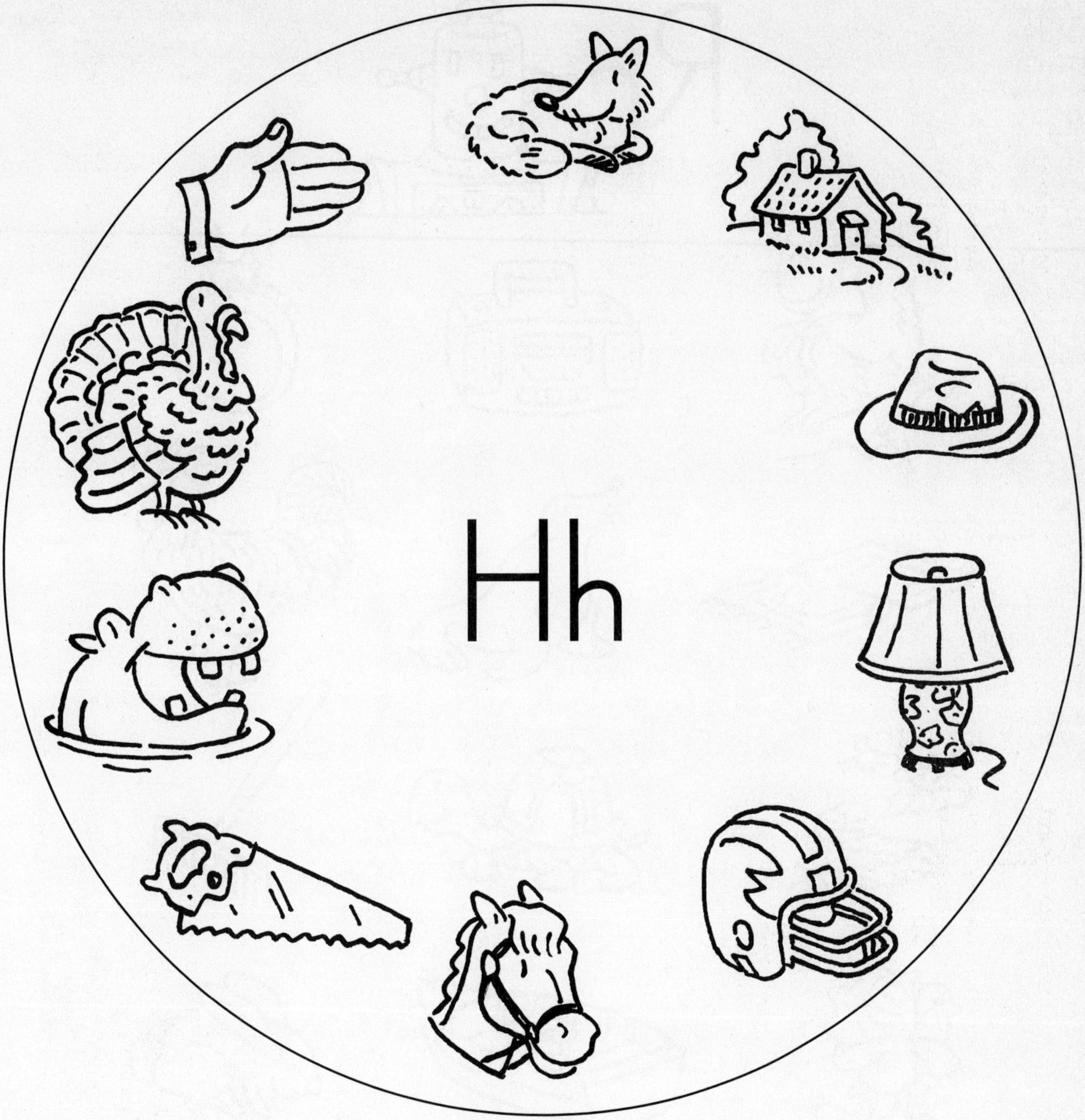

Hh

Directions: Draw lines connecting the letters in the middle with the pictures on the circle that begin with *h*.

Home Activity: Help your child make picture cards and sort the pictures by beginning sounds.

Name ____________________

Circle.

Rr

Directions: Circle the pictures whose names begin like *robot*.

Home Activity: Ask your child to pick out toys he or she has that begin with *r*.

Name ______________________________

Circle.

1. Rr

2. Rr

3. Rr

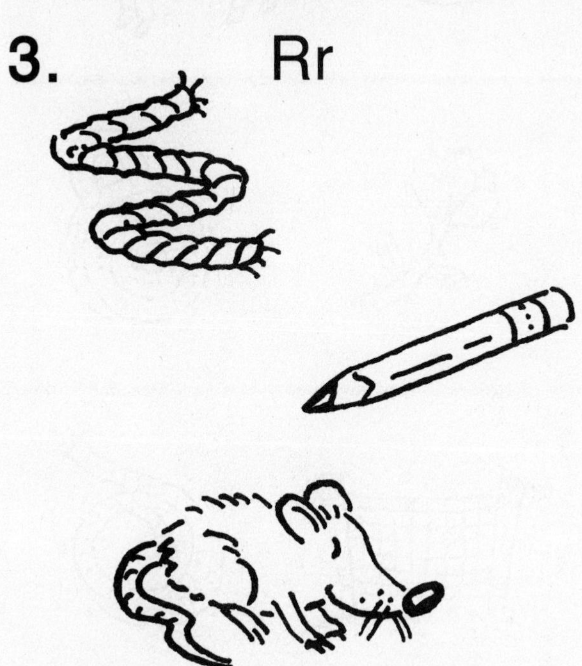

4. Rr

Directions: In each box, circle the pictures whose names begin with *r*.

Home Activity: Have your child tell a story about a robot and use words that begin with *r*.

Name ______________________________

Color.

1. r

2. r

 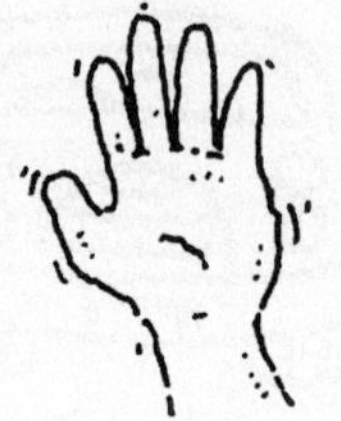 

3. r

4. r

5. r

  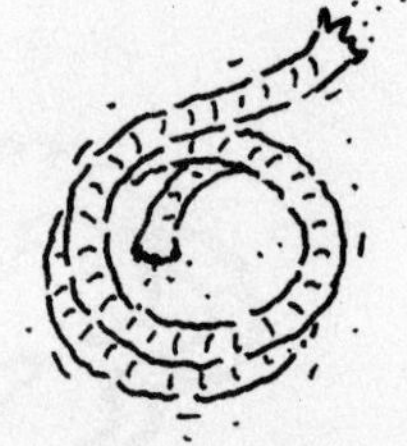

Directions: In each row, color the picture that begins like *robot*.

Home Activity: Help your child find pictures that begin with *r* and paste them on a sheet of paper labeled *r*.

Name ______________________________

Draw lines.

Rr

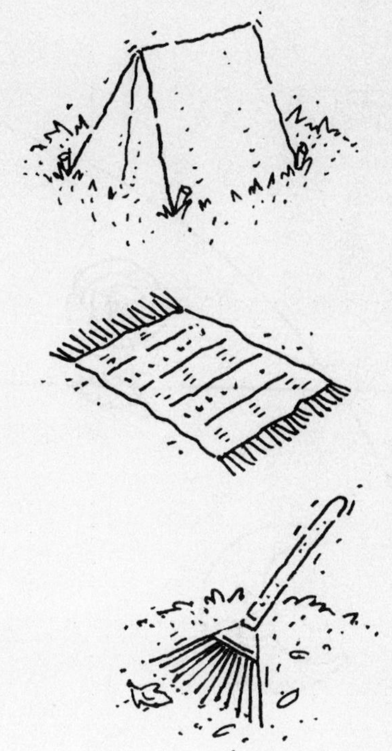

Rr

Directions: Draw lines from the letters to the pictures that begin with that sound.

Home Activity: Say the word *rabbit* and ask your child to name other words that begin like *rabbit*.

Name ______________________

Draw lines.

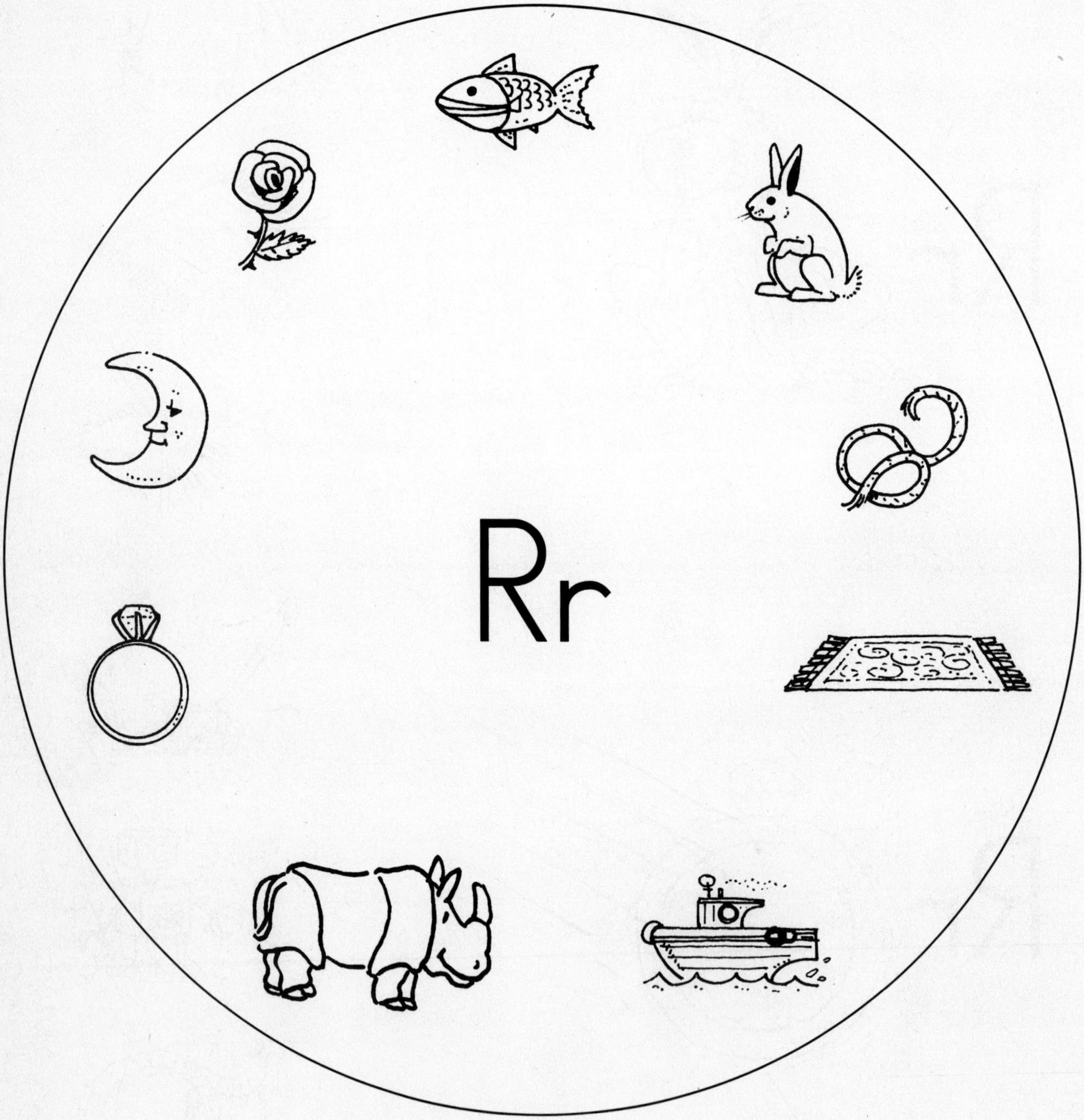

Rr

Directions: Draw lines connecting the letters in the middle with the pictures on the circle that begin with *r*.

Home Activity: Help your child make a paper ring with an *r* on top. Then have your child look for words that begin like *ring*.

Name ______________________________

Circle.

L l

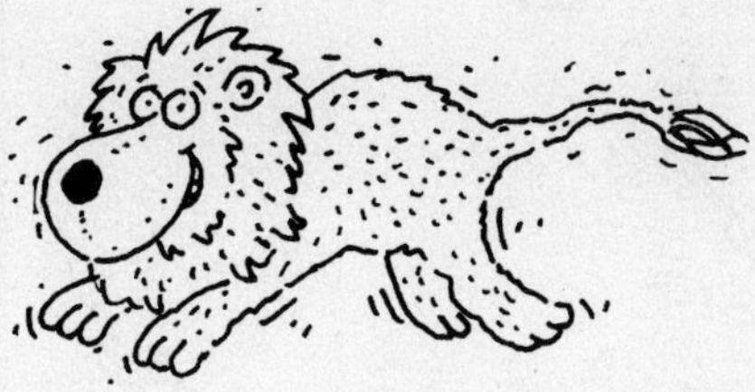

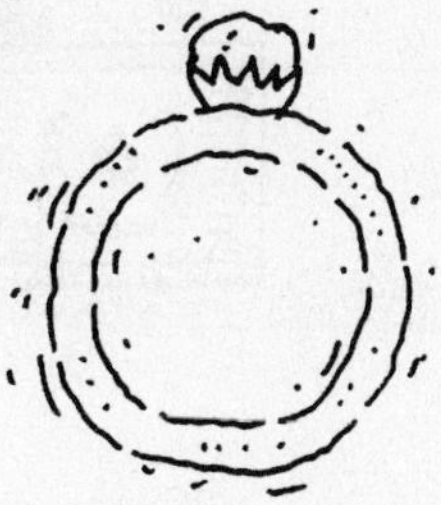

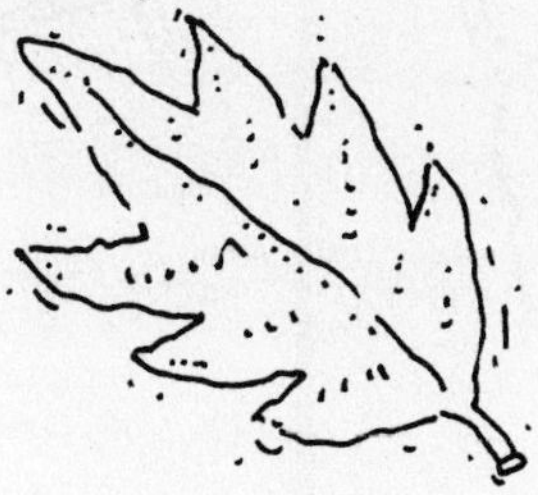

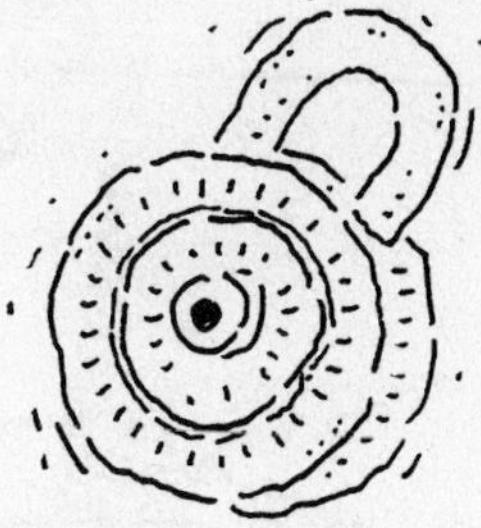

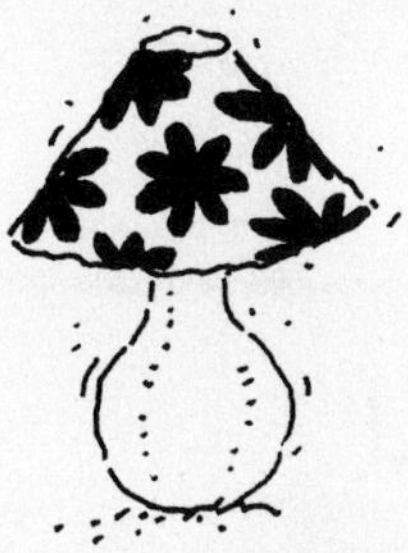

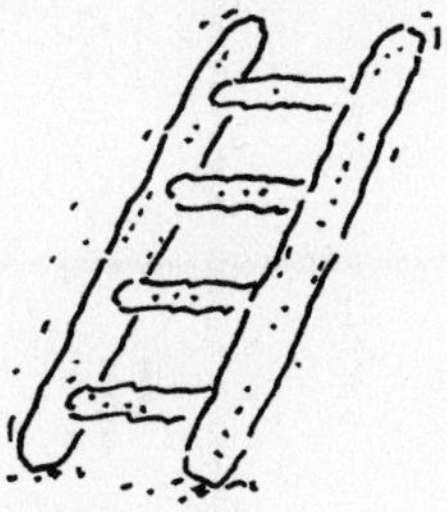

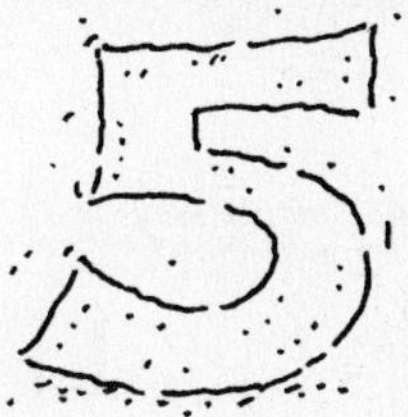

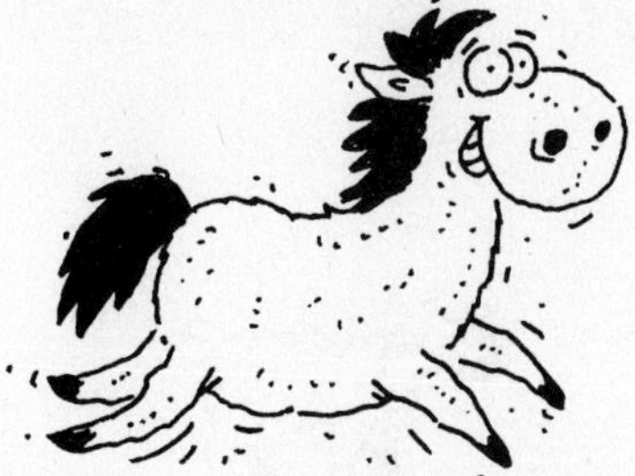

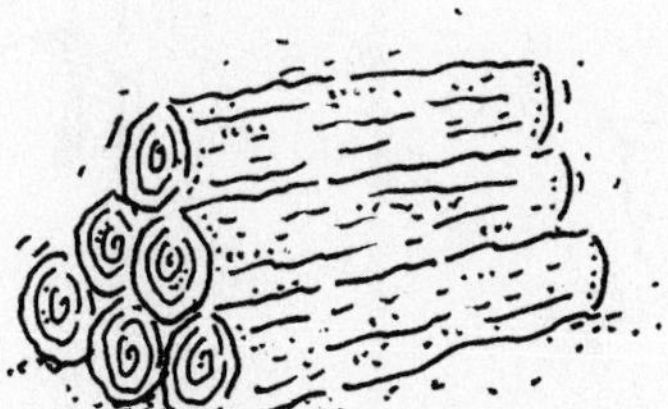

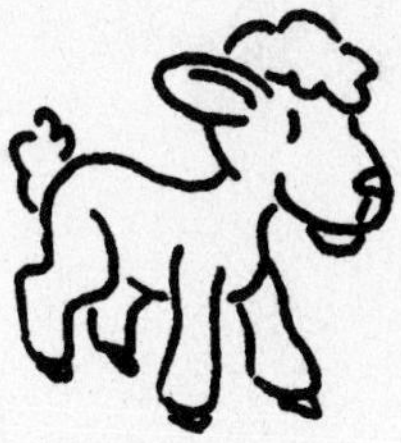

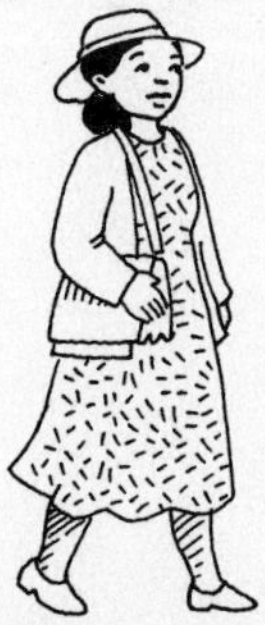

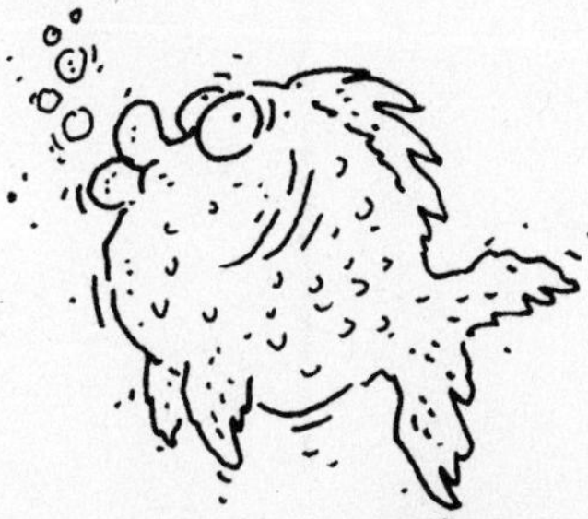

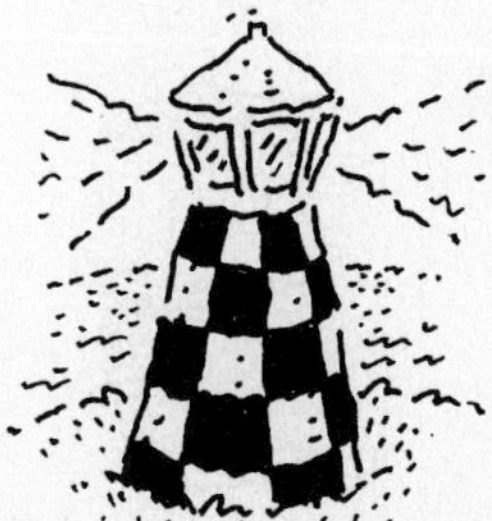

Directions: Circle the pictures whose names begin like *lion*.

Home Activity: Write a large *Ll*. Have your child decorate the letters with pictures of things that begin with *l*.

Name ____________________

Circle.

1. Ll

2. Ll

3. Ll

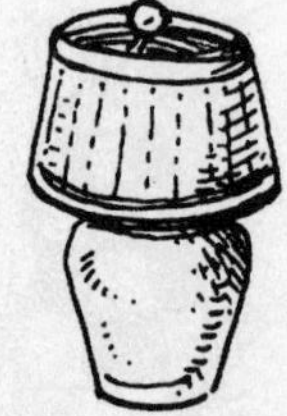

4. Ll

Directions: In each box, circle the pictures whose names begin with *l*.

Home Activity: Point to an *l* picture and have your child name a rhyming word.

Name ______________________________

Color.

1. l

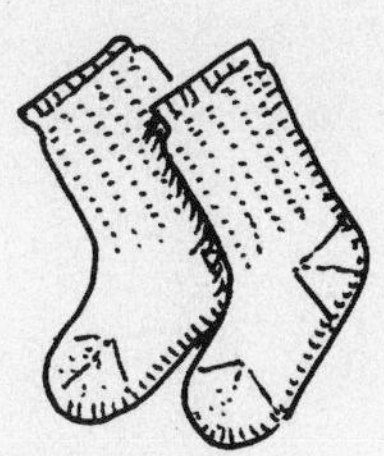  

2. l

3. l

 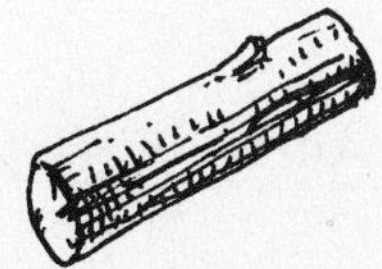 

4. l

 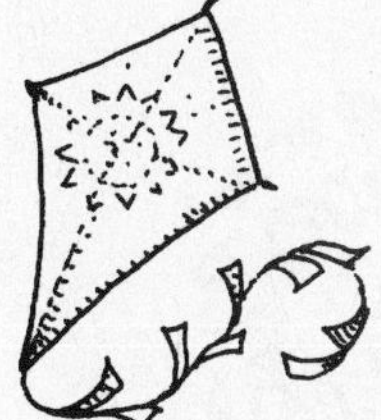 

5. l

Directions: In each row, color the picture that begins like *lion*.

Home Activity: Help your child make up two-word phrases with words that begin with *l—lucky lamb*, *little lion*.

Name ______________________

Draw lines.

Ll 

Ll 

Directions: Draw lines from the letters to the pictures that begin with that sound.

Home Activity: Read a story and have your child name the words that begin with *l*.

Name ______________________________

Draw lines.

Ll

6

2

Directions: Draw lines connecting the letters in the middle with the pictures on the circle that begin with *l*.

Home Activity: Say words and have your child roar like a *lion* each time you say a word that begins with *l*.

Name ______________________

Circle.

Dd

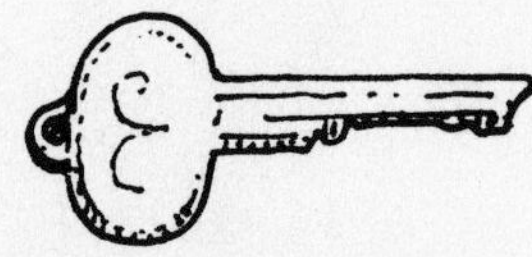

Directions: Circle the pictures whose names begin like *duck.*

Home Activity: Ask your child to think of other words that begin with *d*.

Name ______________________________

Circle.

1. Dd

2. Dd

3. Dd

4. Dd

Directions: In each box, circle the pictures whose names begin with *d*.

Home Activity: Give riddle clues to words that begin with *d—It lives in the woods. (deer)* Ask your child to answer the riddles.

Name ______________________

Color.

1. d

  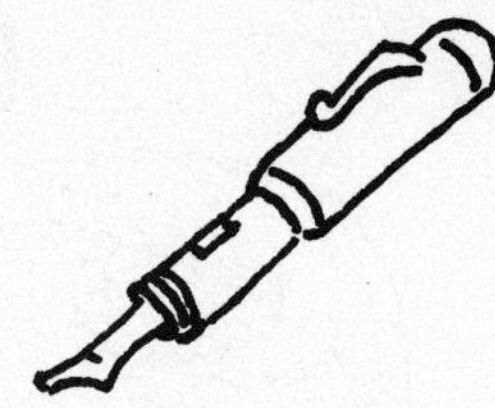

2. d

3. d

  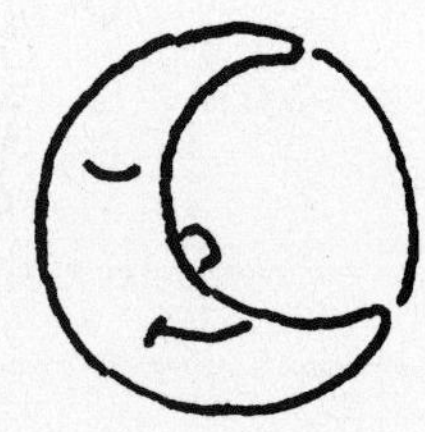

4. d

5. d

Directions: In each row, color the picture that begins like *duck*.

Home Activity: Help your child think of animals whose names begin with *d*. *(dog, duck, deer, donkey)*

Name ______________________________

Draw lines.

Dd

Dd

Directions: Draw lines from the letters to the pictures that begin with that sound.

Home Activity: Write *Dd* on a sheet of paper and have your child draw pictures of things that begin with *d*.

Name ____________________

Draw lines.

Dd

Directions: Draw lines connecting the letters in the middle with the pictures on the circle that begin with *d*.

Home Activity: Ask your child to make *d* rhyming words for these words—*luck, log, lime, fish, big, hid.*

Name ______________________________

Circle.

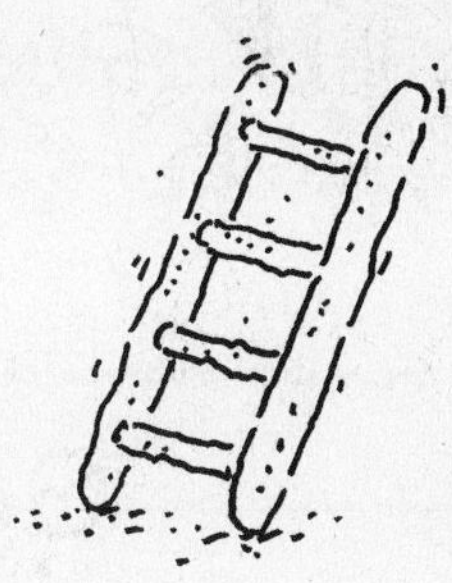

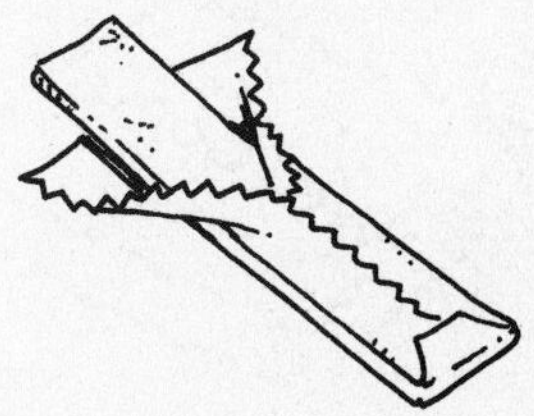

Directions: Circle the pictures whose names begin like *goat*.

Home Activity: Ask your child to think of other words that begin with *g*.

Name ______________________

Circle.

1. Gg

2. Gg

3. Gg

4. Gg

Directions: In each box, circle the pictures whose names begin with *g*.

Home Activity: Read a story and have your child listen for words that begin with *g*.

Name ____________________

Color.

1. g

2. g

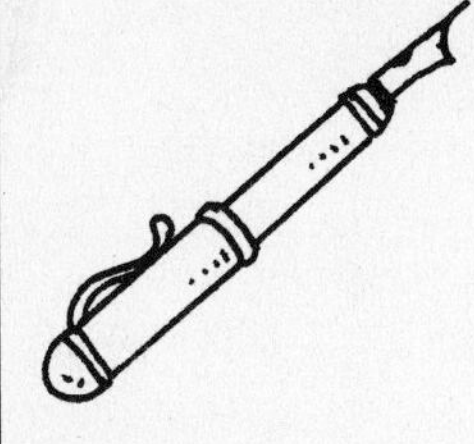  

3. g

4. g

 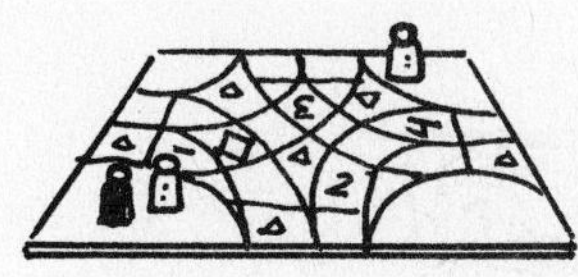 

5. g

 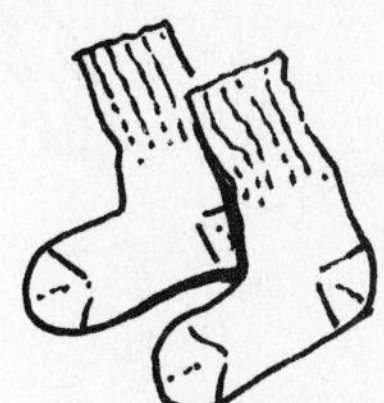 

Directions: In each row, color the picture that begins like *goat.*

Home Activity: Have your child name *g* words to finish this sentence: *Get a* ____.

Name ______________________

Draw lines.

Gg

9

5

Directions: Draw lines connecting the letters in the middle with the pictures on the circle that begin with *g*.

Home Activity: Say three words—*good, laugh, gallop*. Have your child name the words that begin with *g*.

Name ______________________________

Draw lines.

g

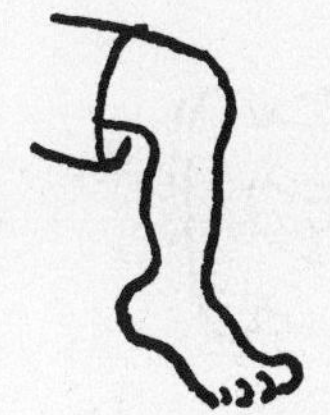

g

Directions: Draw lines to match the pictures whose names end with the letter *g*.

Home Activity: Write a word—*pig*. Have your child say the word and underline the letter *g*.

Name ______________________________

Color.

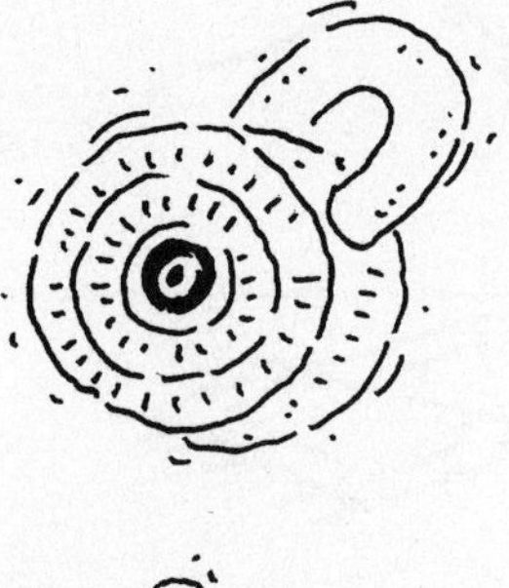

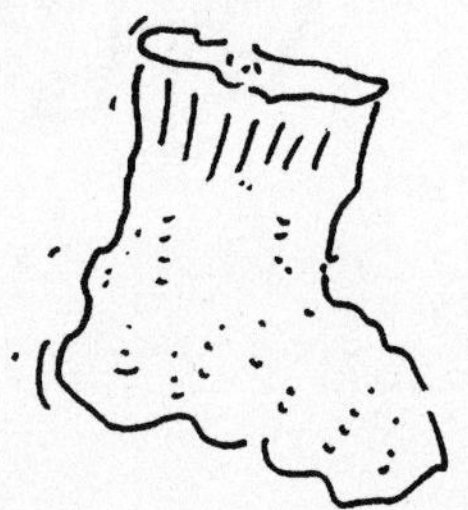

Directions: Color the pictures whose names have the short *o* sound.

Home Activity: Have your child change vowel sounds to short *o* to make new words from *map, tip, luck, cat.*

Name ______________________________

Draw a line.

1.

2.

3.

4.

Directions: Draw a line to match pictures with the short *o* sound.

Home Activity: Point to a short *o* picture and have your child name a rhyming word.

Name ______________________

Circle.

1.

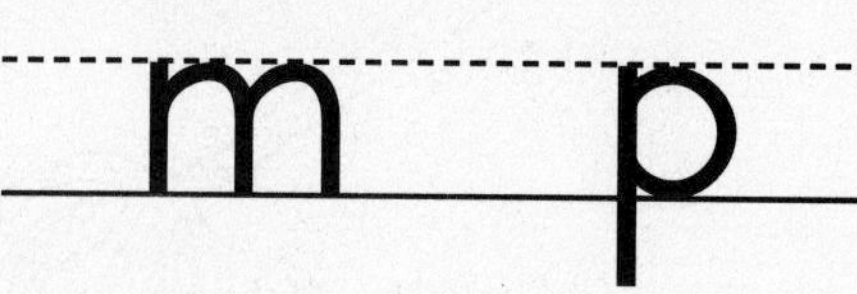

2.

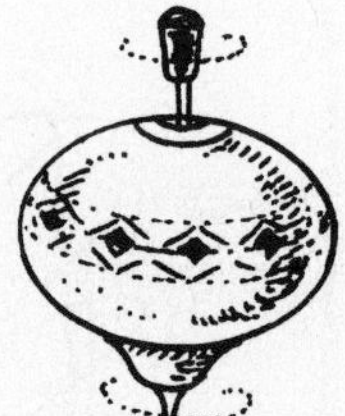

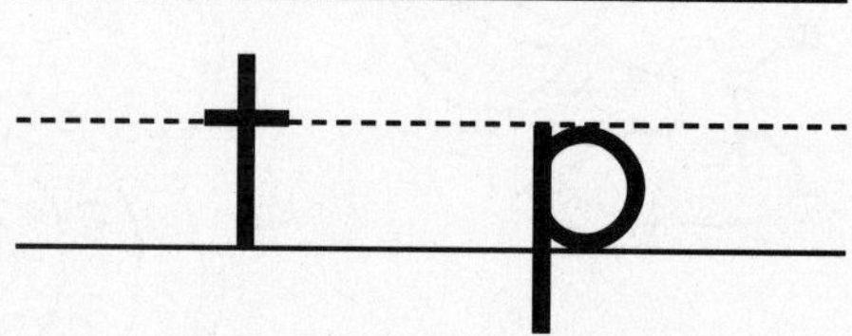

3.

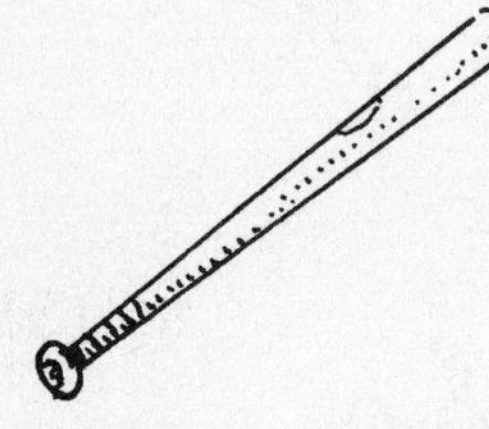

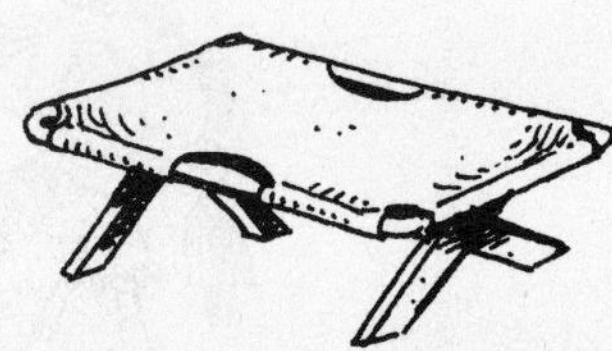

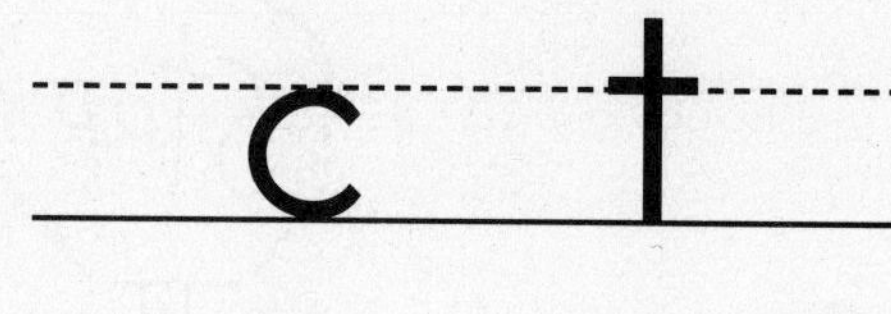

4.

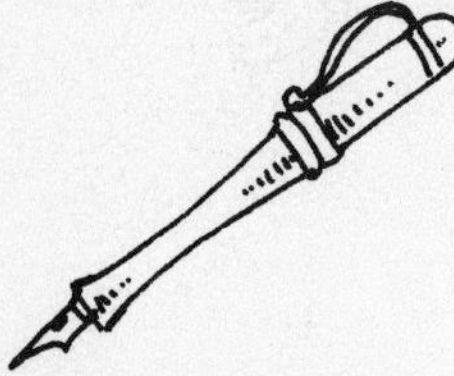

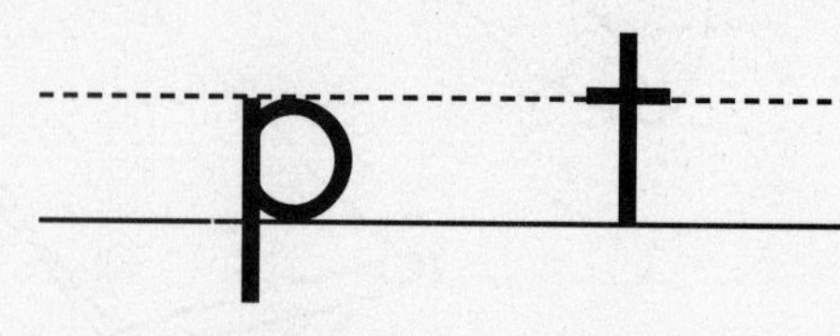

Directions: In each row, circle the picture with the short *o* sound. Write the letter to finish the picture name.

Home Activity: Make letter cards for *m, p, t, c,* and *o*. Help your child arrange the letters to make the words on this page.

Name ______________________

Color.

1.

hot

2.

dot

3.

hop

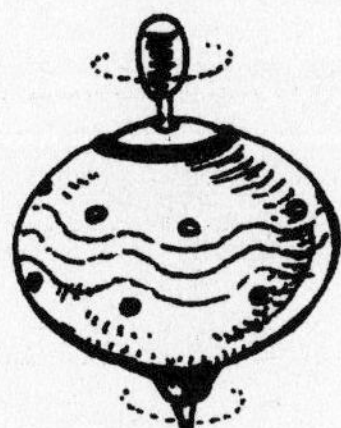

4.

mop

Directions: In each box, color the picture that rhymes with the word at the top of the box.

Home Activity: Write the word *hot*. Help your child write words that rhyme with *hot*. Repeat with *hop*.

Name ____________________

Circle.

1. top

2. pot

3. cot

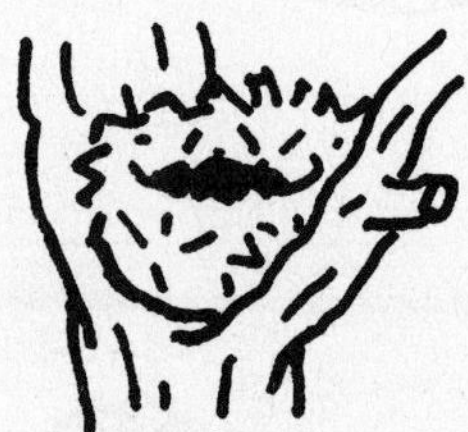

4. hop

5. mop

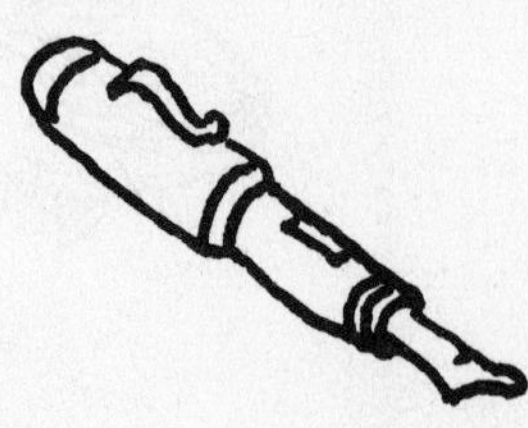

Directions: In each row, circle the picture the word names.

Home Activity: Say one of the words on the page and have your child point to the word.

Name ______________________________

Circle.

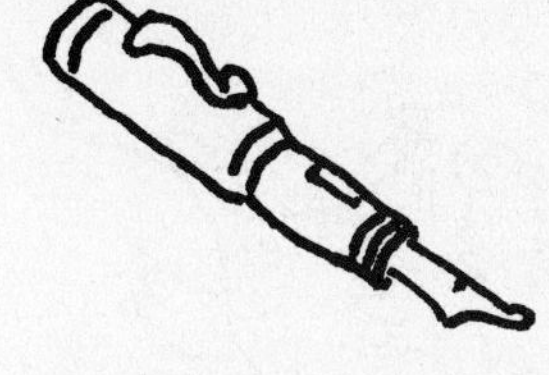

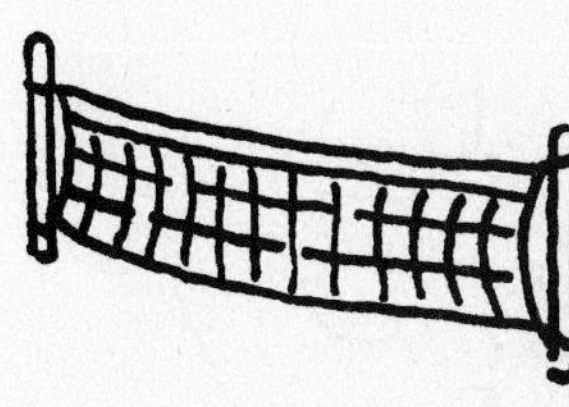

Directions: Circle the pictures whose names begin like *kangaroo*.

Home Activity: Give a clue about a *k* word and ask your child to name the word—*being nice* (*kind*).

Name ______________________________

Circle.

1. Kk

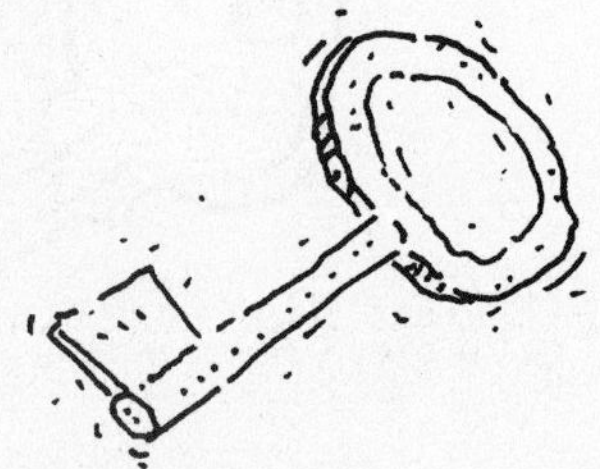

2. Kk

3. Kk

4. Kk

Directions: In each box, circle the picture whose name begins with *k*.

Home Activity: Help your child make up tongue twisters with *k* words—*Kitten kicks a kettle to Kangaroo.*

Name ____________________

Color.

1. k

2. k

3. k

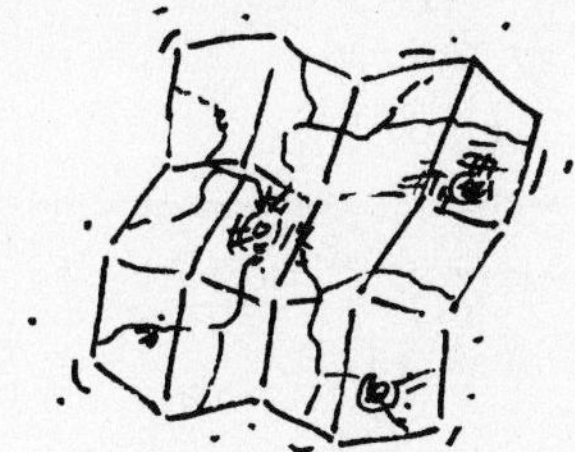

4. k

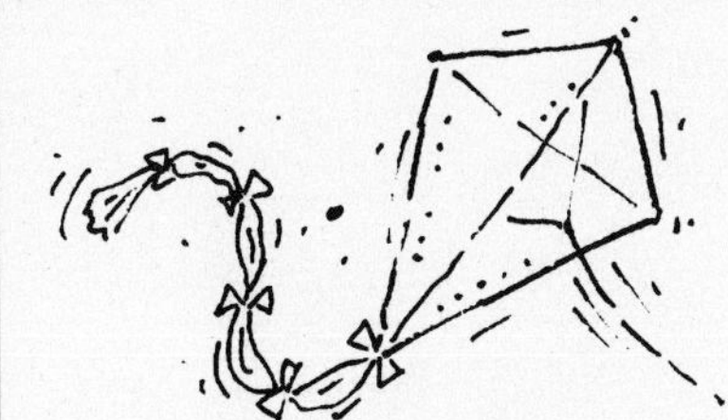

5. k

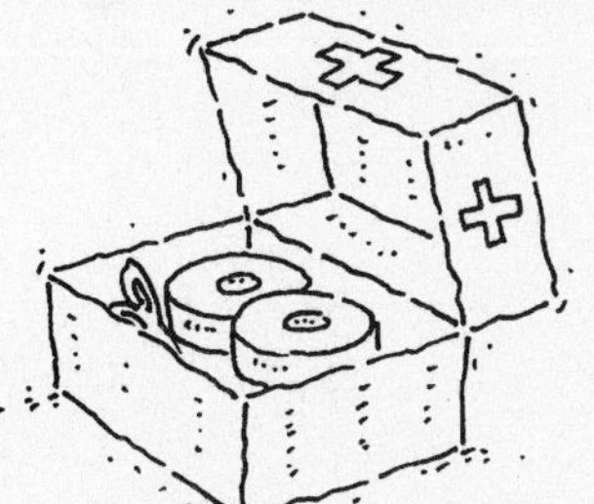

Directions: In each row, color the picture that begins like *kangaroo*.

Home Activity: Show a key. Have your child point to the key if a word you say begins like *key*.

Name ______________________

Draw lines.

Kk 

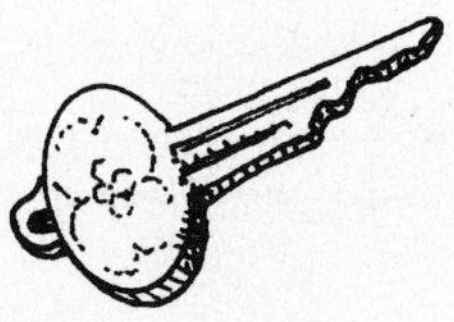

Kk 

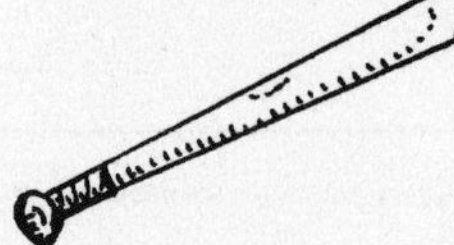

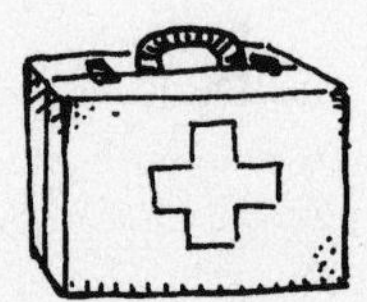

Directions: Draw lines from the letters to the pictures that begin with that sound.

Home Activity: Help your child draw pictures of things that begin with *k*.

Name ________________________________

Draw lines.

Kk

Directions: Draw lines connecting the letters in the middle with the pictures on the circle that begin with *k*.

Home Activity: Ask your child to name *k* words that rhyme with *pick, hit, mitten, ring, bite.*

Name ______________________________

Circle.

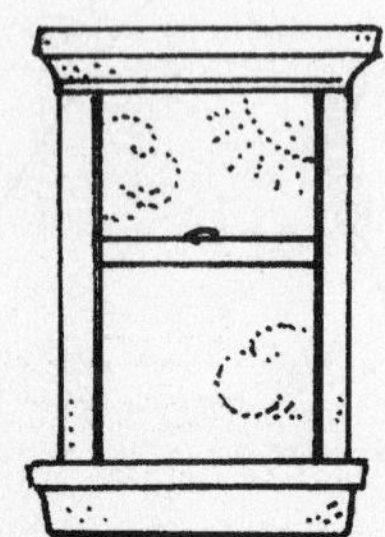

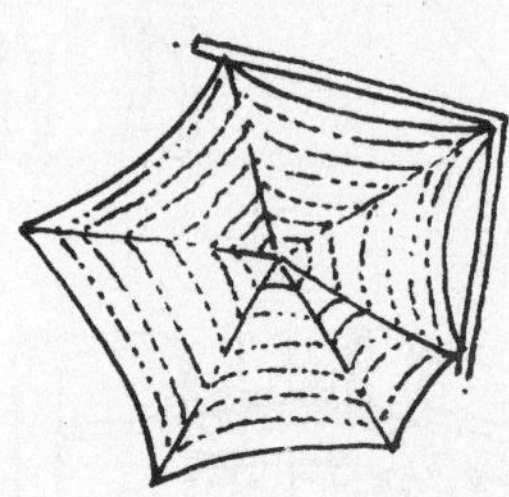

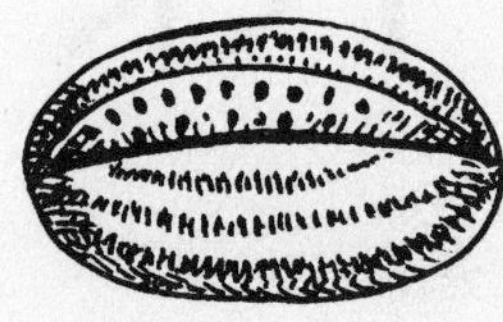

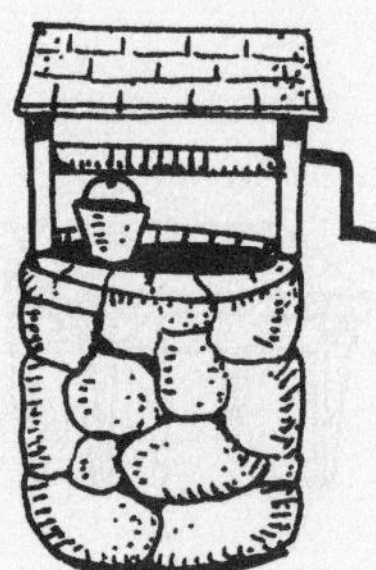

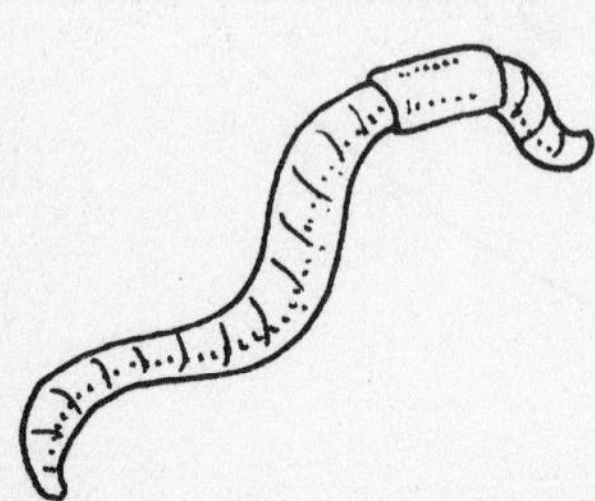

Directions: Circle the pictures whose names begin like *wagon*.

Home Activity: Draw a large window. Have your child say words that begin like *window* and write a *w* on the window for each word.

Name ______________________________

Circle.

1. Ww

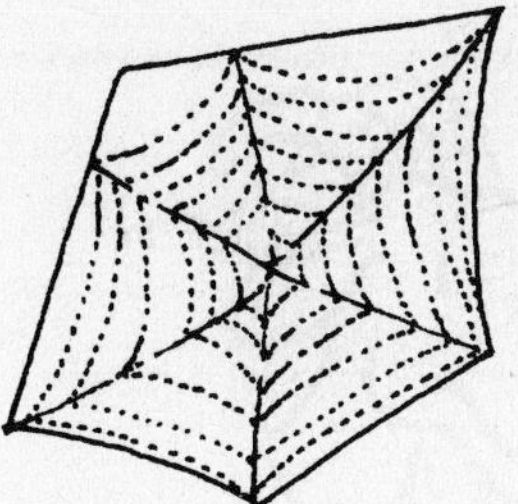

2. Ww

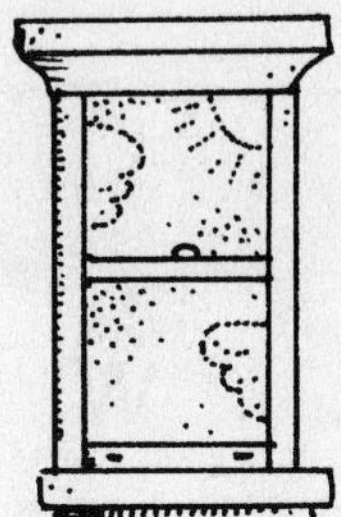

3. Ww

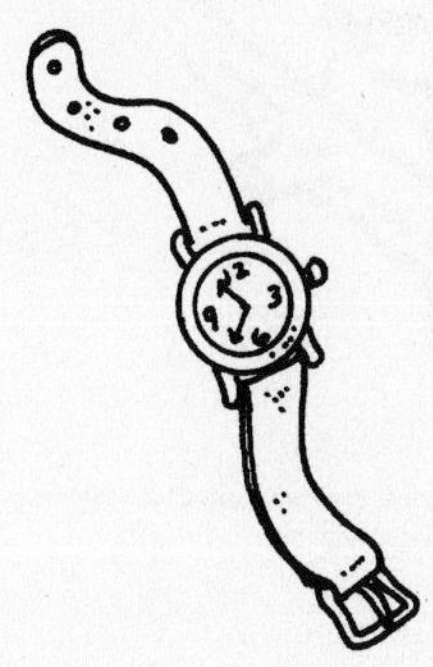

4. Ww

Directions: In each box, circle the picture whose name begins with *w*.

Home Activity: As you say different words, ask your child to identify those that begin with *w*.

Name ______________________

Color.

1. w

2. w

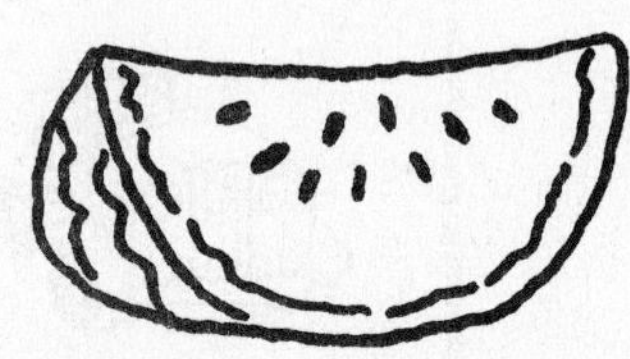

3. w

4. w

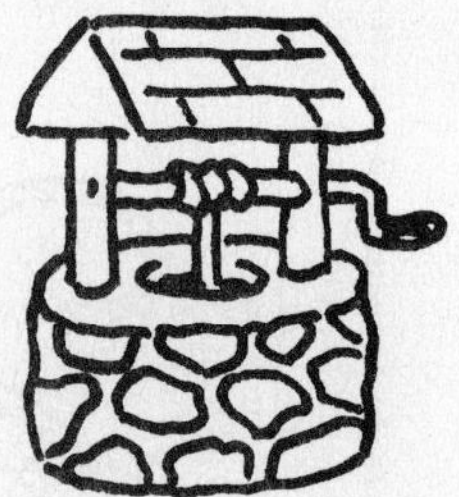

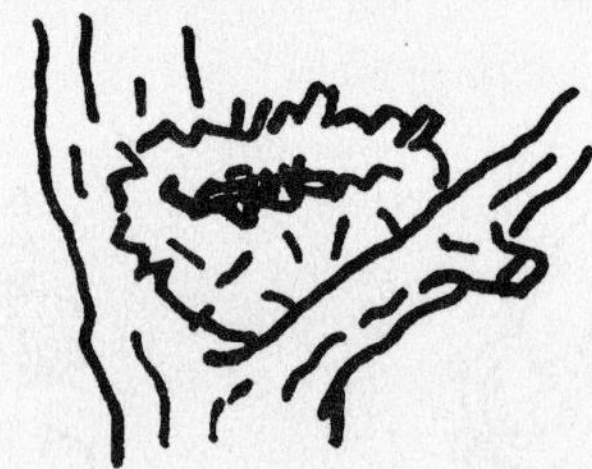

5. w

Directions: In each row, color the picture that begins like *wagon*.

Home Activity: Point to a picture and ask your child to write the letter for the beginning sound.

Name ______________________________

Draw lines.

Ww

Ww

Directions: Draw lines from the letters to the pictures that begin with that sound.

Home Activity: Say *tire—wire*. Ask your child to name the word that begins with *w*.

Name ______________________________

Draw lines.

Ww

Directions: Draw lines connecting the letters in the middle with the pictures on the circle that begin with *w*.

Home Activity: Ask your child to draw pictures of things that begin with *w*.

Name ________________________________

Circle.

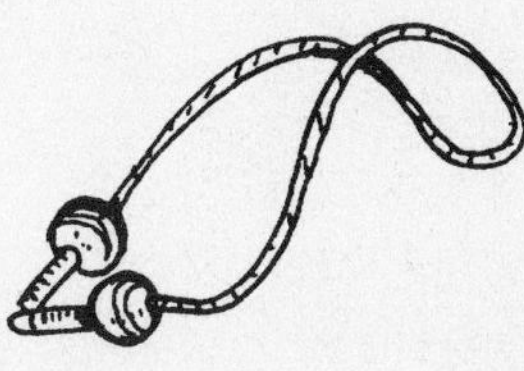

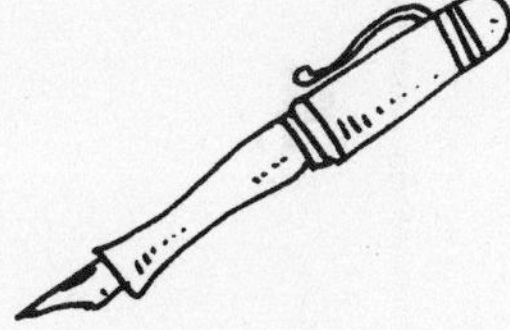

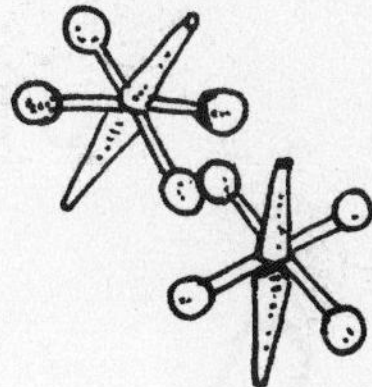

Directions: Circle the pictures whose names begin like *jeep*.

Home Activity: Say words. Ask your child to jump each time you say a word that begins with *j*.

Name ______________________________

Circle.

1. Jj

2. Jj

3. Jj

4. Jj

Directions: In each box, circle the picture whose name begins with *j*.

Home Activity: Draw a large jar on a sheet of paper. Have your child write *j*'s on the jar and say words that begin like *jar*.

Name ______________________

Circle.

1. j

2. j

3. j

4. j

5. j

Directions: In each row, circle the picture that begins like *jeep*.

Home Activity: Help your child make up two-word phrases with words that begin with *j—jumpy jet*.

Name ______________________

Draw lines.

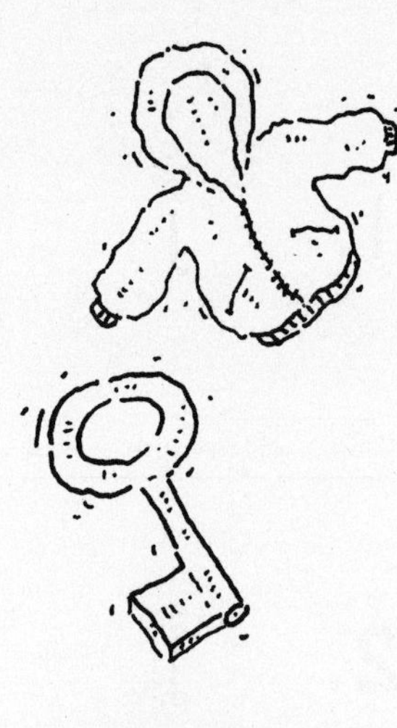

Jj

Jj

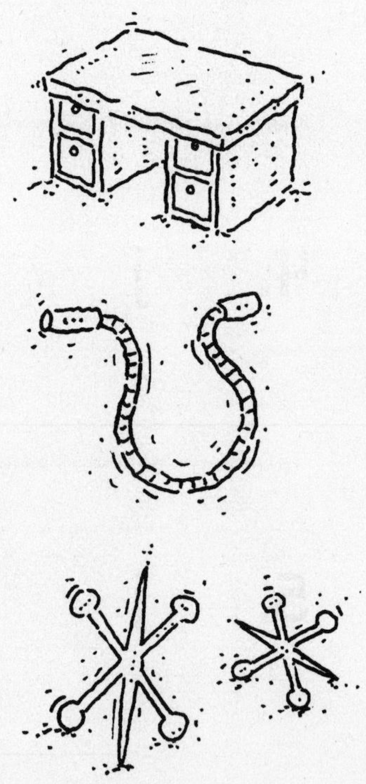

Directions: Draw lines from the letters to the pictures that begin with that sound.

Home Activity: Help your child create a jump rope rhyme—*Jack and Jill, jump to the hill. They jump, jump, jump.*

Name ______________________________

Draw lines.

J j

Directions: Draw lines connecting the letters in the middle with the pictures on the circle that begin with *j*.

Home Activity: Have your child answer riddles about *j* words. *Something that flies* (*jet*). *Kind of car* (*jeep*).

Name ______________________________

Circle.

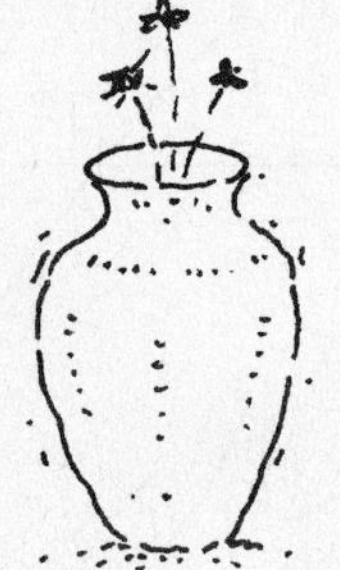

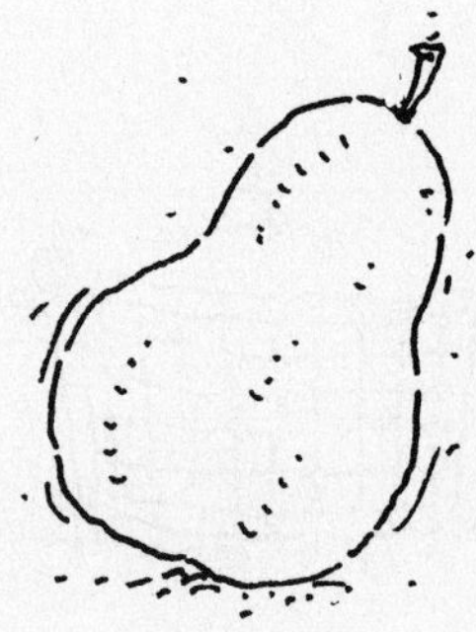

Directions: Circle the pictures whose names begin like *violin*.

Home Activity: Help your child make a valentine and write the letter *v* on the valentine for each *v* word he or she names.

Name ____________________

Circle.

1. Vv

2. Vv

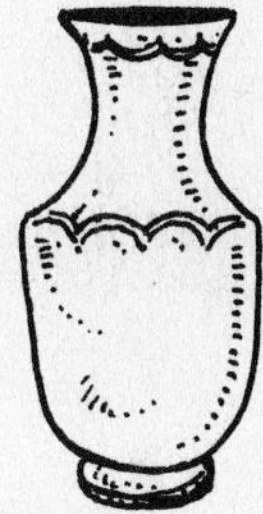

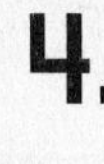

3. Vv

4. Vv

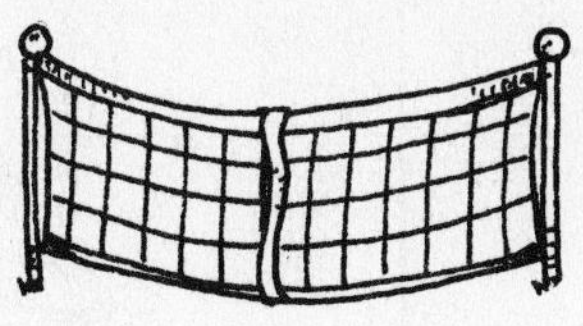

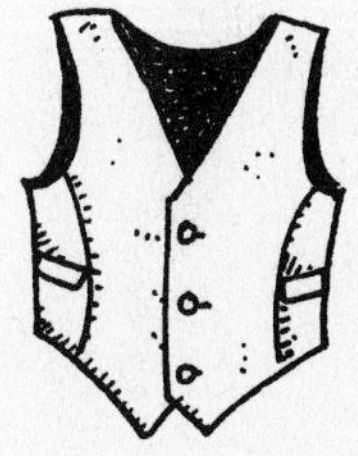

Directions: In each box, circle the picture whose name begins with *v*.

Home Activity: Say a word and have your child pretend to play a violin if the word begins with *v*.

Name ____________________

Color.

1. v

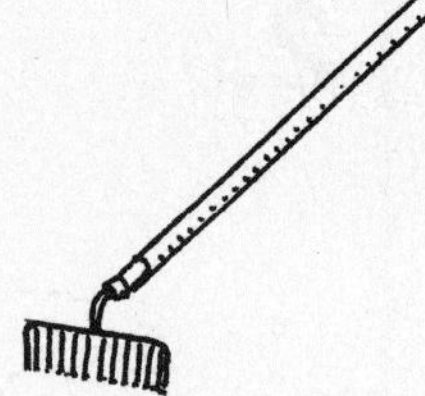

2. v

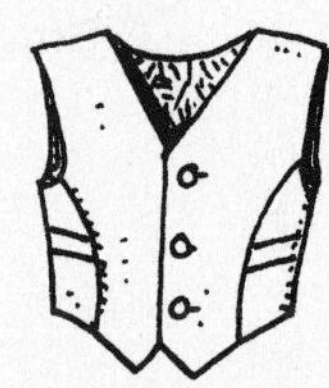

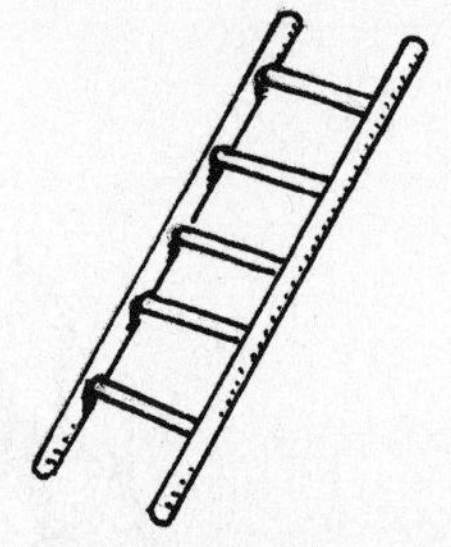

3. v

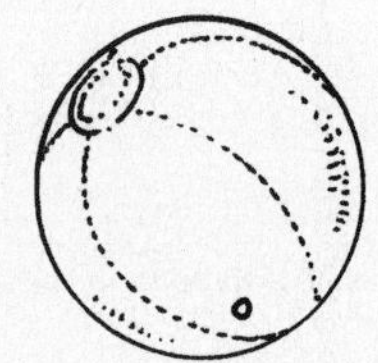

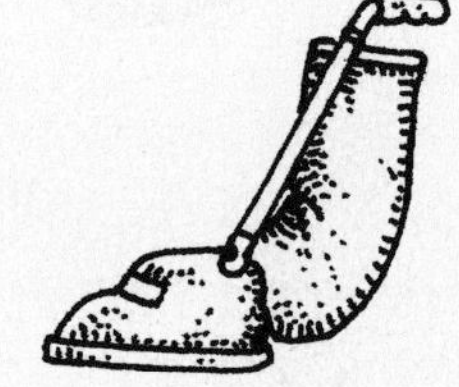

4. v

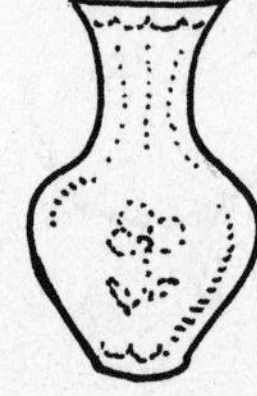

5. v

Directions: In each row, color the picture that begins like *violin*.

Home Activity: Help your child say tongue twisters with *v* words—*Vera Vase visited Van the Violin.*

Name ______________________

Draw lines.

Directions: Draw lines from the letters to the pictures that begin with that sound.

Home Activity: Have your child change the beginning sound to make *v* words: *line* (*vine*), *best* (*vest*), *can* (*van*), *rein* (*vein*).

Name ____________________

Draw lines.

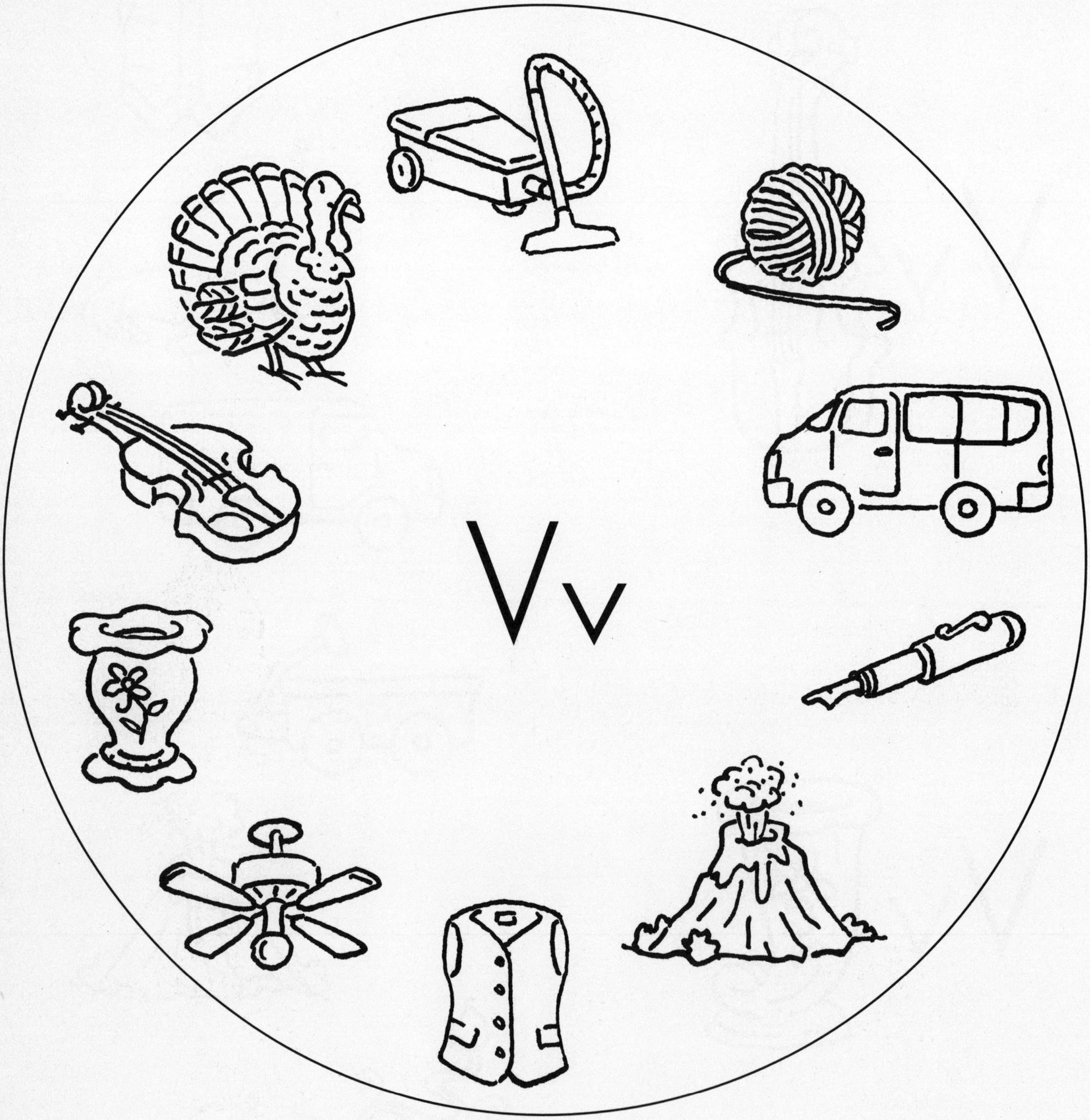

Vv

Directions: Draw lines connecting the letters in the middle with the pictures on the circle that begin with *v*.

Home Activity: Point to a picture on the page. Have your child name the picture and the letter for the beginning sound.

Name ___________________________

Circle.

q 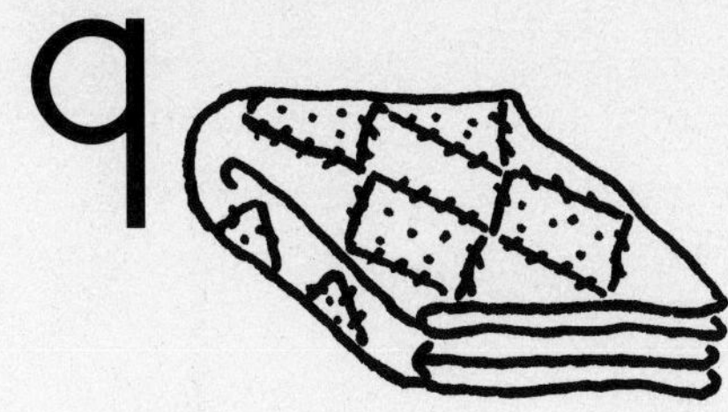

Directions: Circle the pictures whose names begin like *quilt*.

Home Activity: Give clues and have your child guess the *q* words. (*quick, quarrel, quit, quite, quiz*)

Name ______________________

Circle.

1. q

2. q

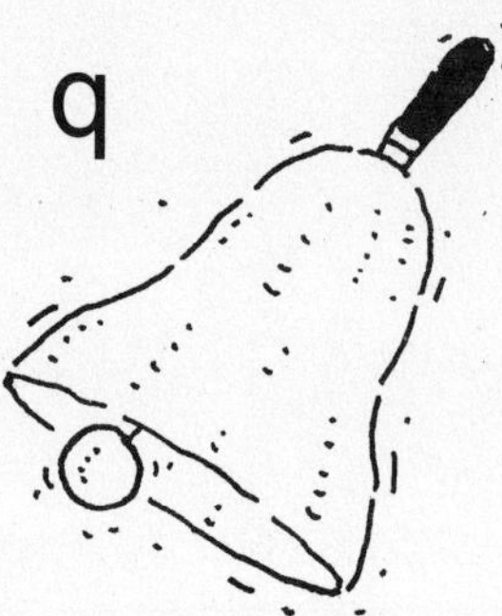

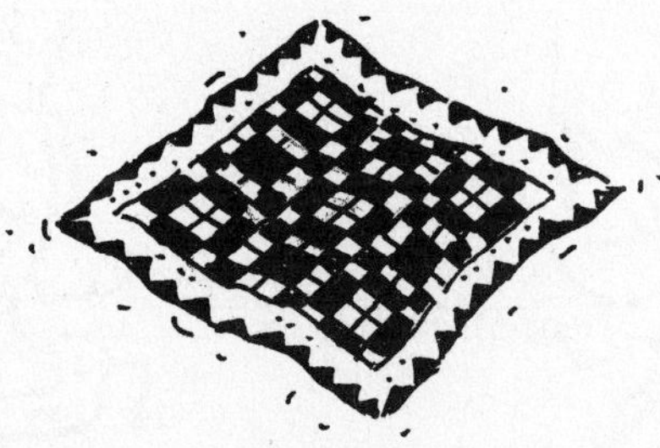

3. q

4. q

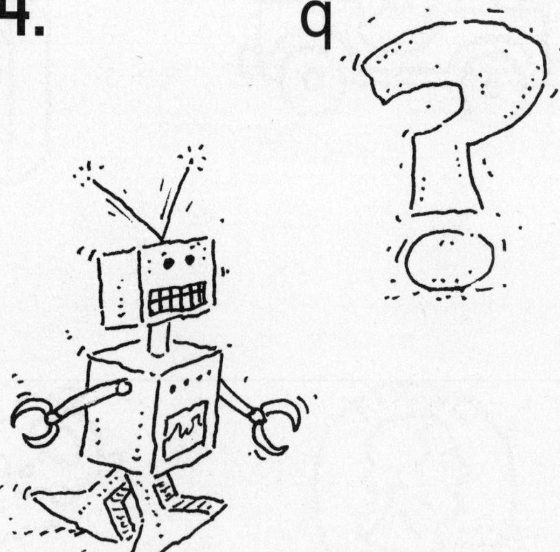

Directions: In each box, circle the picture whose name begins with *q*.

Home Activity: As you say different words, ask your child to identify those that begin with *q*.

Name ______________________________

Color.

1. q  

2. q  

3. q  

4. q  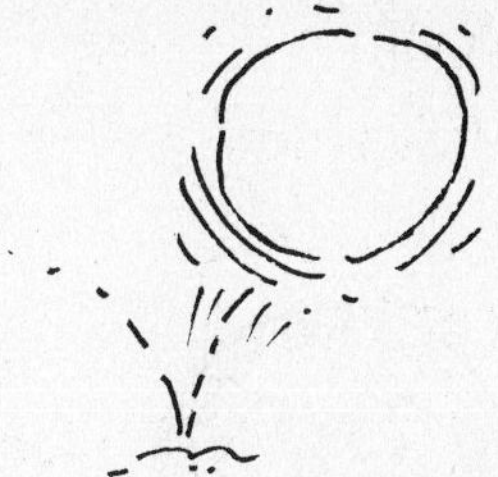

5. q  

Directions: In each row, color the picture that begins with *q*.

Home Activity: Help your child write several *q* words.

Name ________________________________

Draw lines.

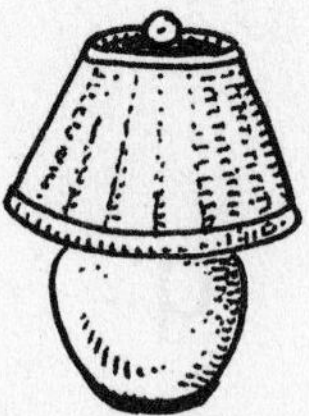

q 

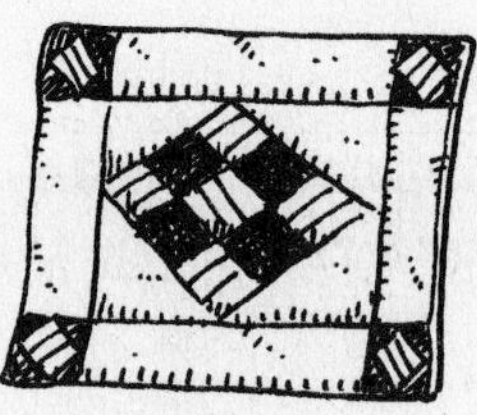

q 

Directions: Draw lines from the letter to the pictures that begin with that sound.

Home Activity: Point to a picture and ask your child to name the beginning letter.

Name ________________________________

Draw lines.

Qq

Directions: Draw lines connecting the letters in the middle with the pictures on the circle that begin with *q*.

Home Activity: Help your child make a *q* rhyming word for these words: *pick* (*quick*), *back* (*quack*), *built* (*quilt*), *seen* (*queen*).

Name ______________________________ Short *e*

Color.

pen 

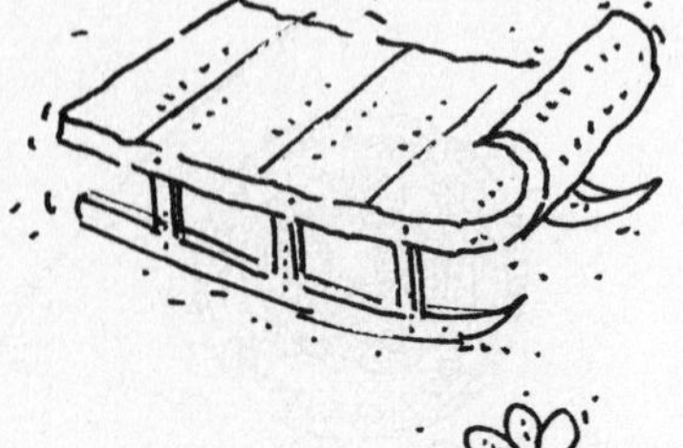

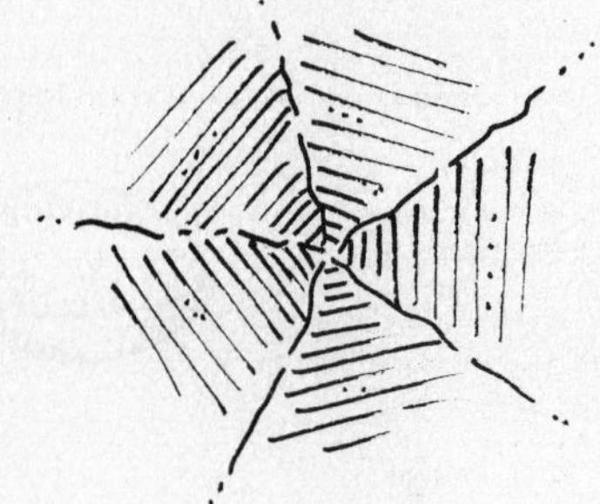

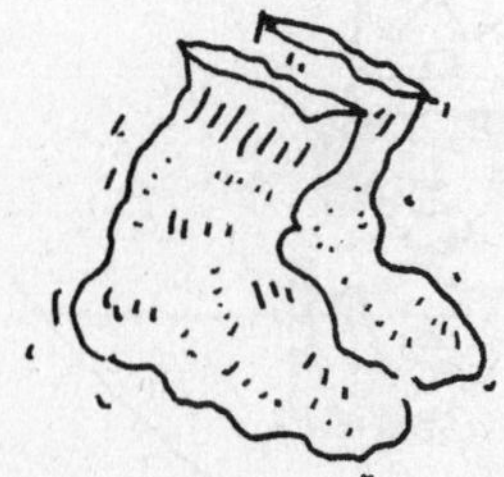

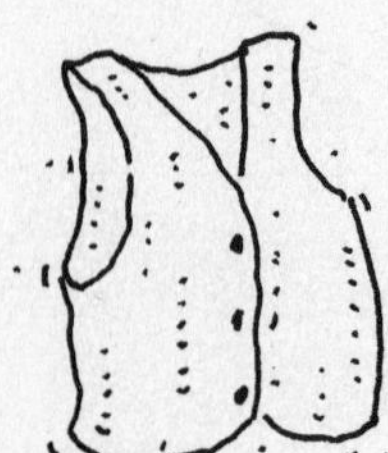

Directions: Color the pictures whose names have the short *e* sound.

Home Activity: Give a clue about a short *e* word and ask your child to name the word—*something to wear.*

Name ______________________

Draw a line.

1.

2.

3.

4.

Directions: Draw a line to match the pictures with the short *e* sound.

Home Activity: Have your child name words that rhyme with *bed—red, fed, Ned, led, wed, Ted, sled.*

Name ______________________

Circle.

1.

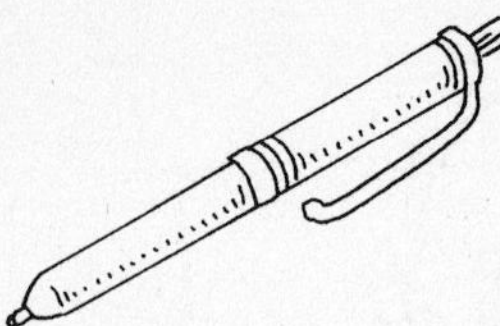

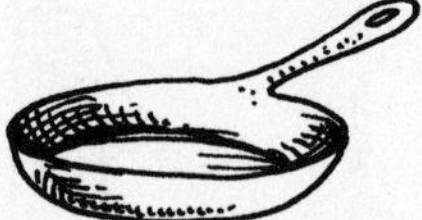

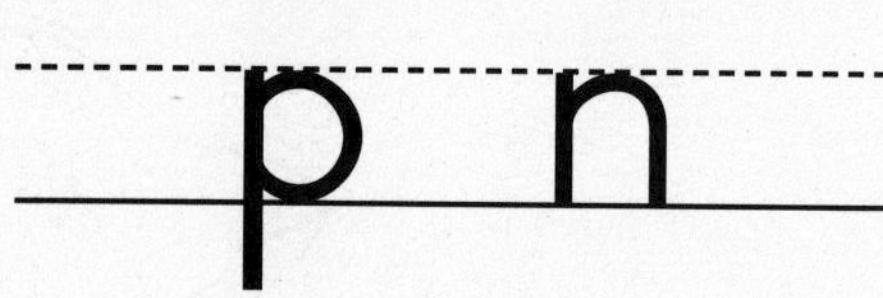

2.

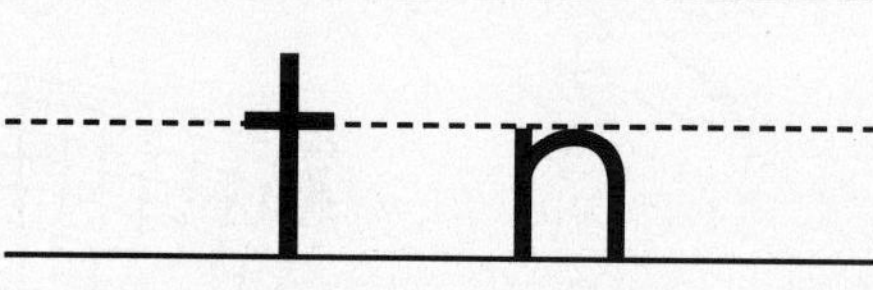

3.

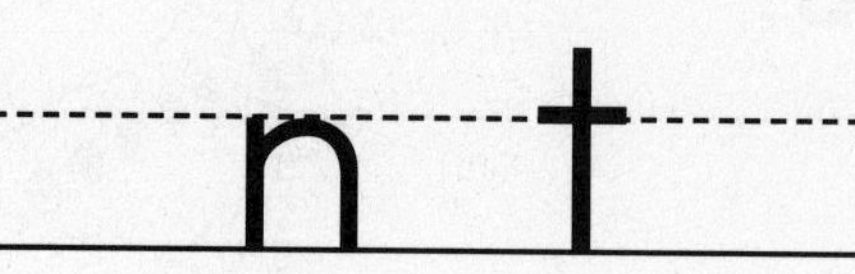

4.

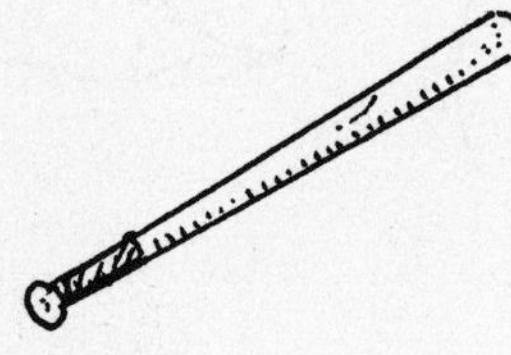

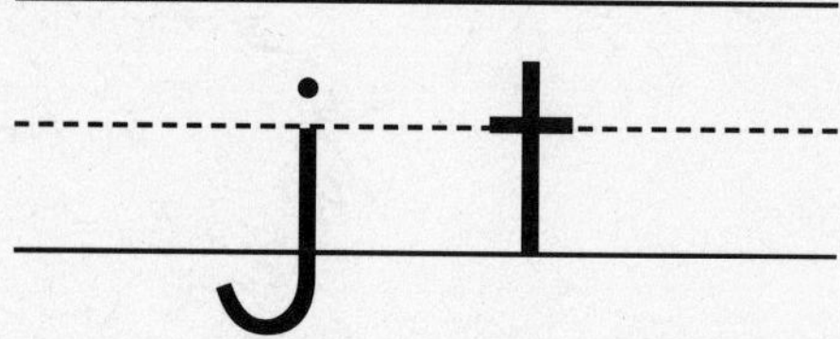

Directions: In each row, circle the picture with the short *e* sound. Write the letter to finish the picture name.

Home Activity: Make letter cards for *p, n, t, j,* and *e*. Help your child arrange the letters to make the words on this page.

Name ______________________________

Color.

1.

vet

2.

pet

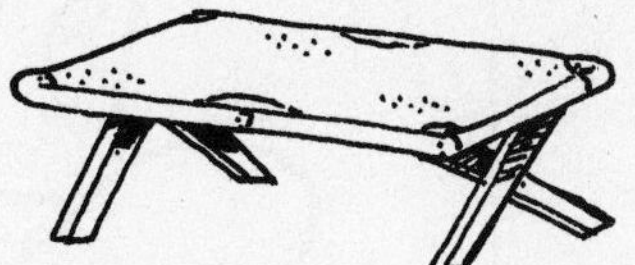

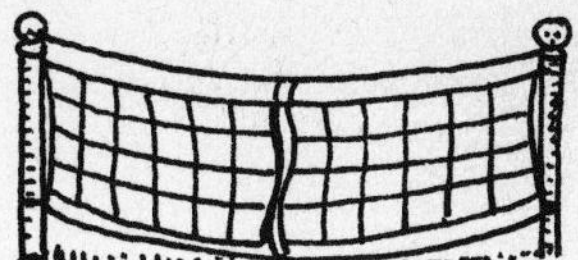

3.

hen

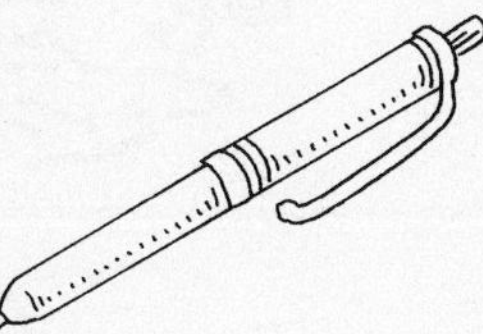

4.

men

10

Directions: In each box, color the picture that rhymes with the word at the top of the box.

Home Activity: Write the word *nest* on a sheet of paper. Help your child write words that rhyme with *nest*.

Name ______________________________

Circle.

1. pet

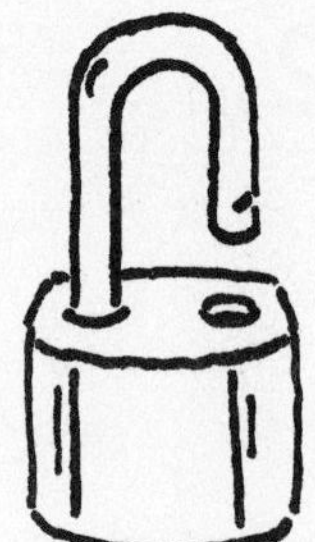

2. net

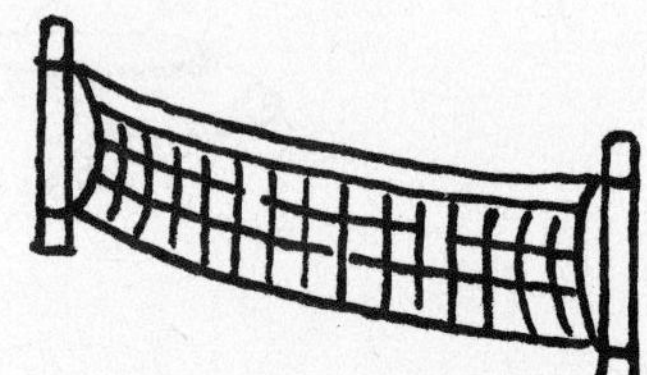

3. jet

4. wet

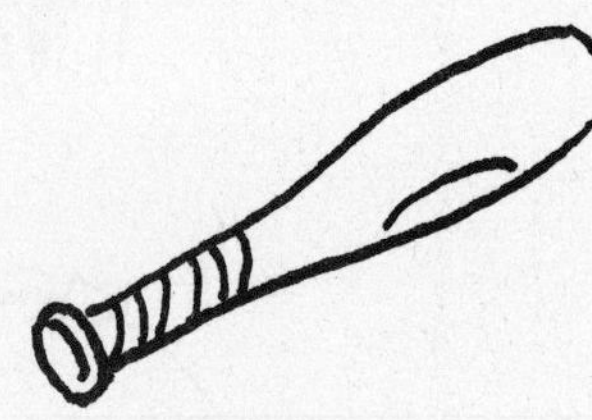

5. vet

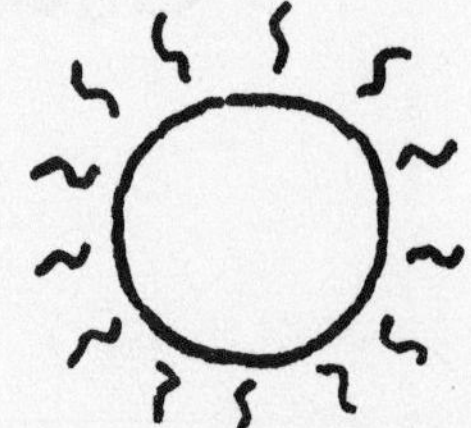

Directions: In each row, circle the picture the word names.

Home Activity: Point to a word on the page and have your child use the word in a sentence.

Name ______________________________

Circle.

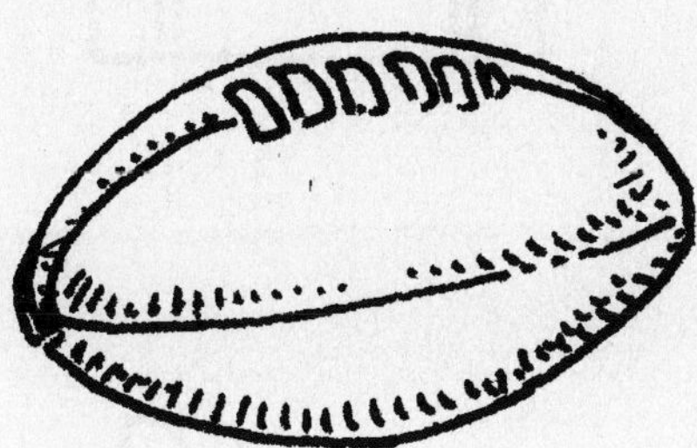

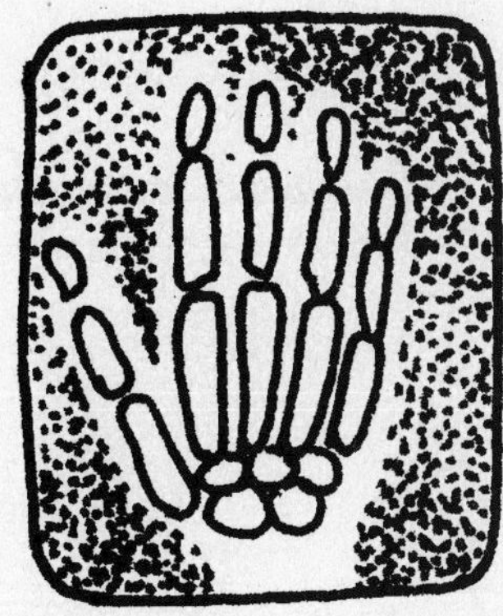

Directions: Circle the picture whose name begins with *x*.

Home Activity: Have your child find items in the kitchen that have words with *x*.

Name ______________________________

Circle.

1. x

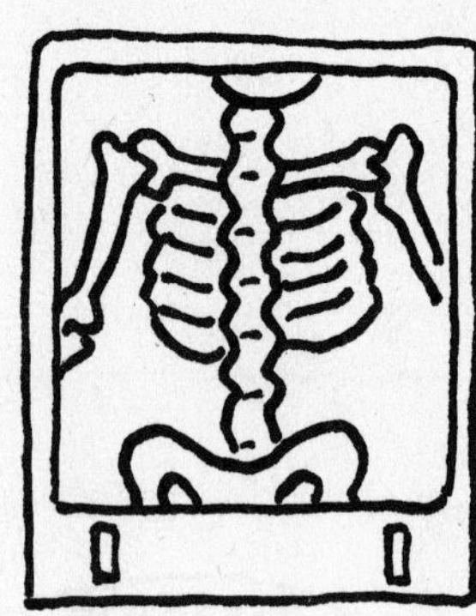

2. x

3. x

Directions: In each row, circle the pictures whose names have an *x*.

Home Activity: Ask your child to think of rhyming words with *x*.

Name ______________________________

Color.

I. x

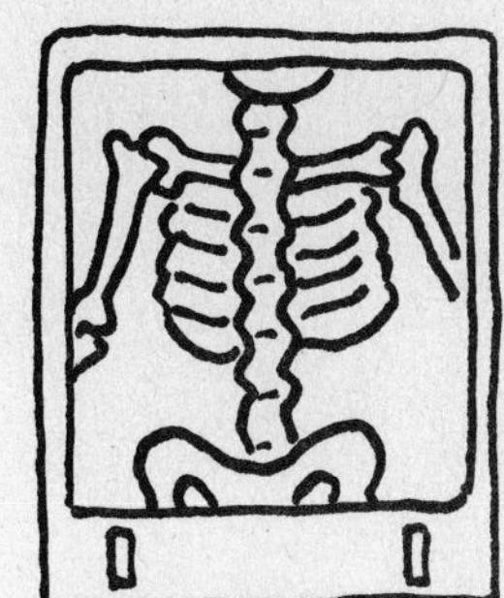

2. x

3. x

4. x

Directions: In each row, color the picture that has an *x*.

Home Activity: Help your child make up phrases using words with *x*— *A fox in a box.*

Name ______________________________

Draw lines.

X

Directions: Draw lines from the letter to the pictures that end with *x*.

Home Activity: Point to a picture and ask your child to name the beginning letter.

Name ______________________________

Draw lines.

Xx

Directions: Draw lines connecting the letters in the middle with the pictures on the circle that have an *x*.

Home Activity: Ask your child to draw pictures of things that have an *x* such as *box, fox,* and *x-ray.*

Name ______________________________

Circle.

Yy

Directions: Circle the pictures whose names begin like *yellow.*

Home Activity: Say words. Ask your child to say "yes" each time you say a word that begins with *y.*

Name ________________________________

Circle.

1. Yy

2. Yy

Directions: Circle the pictures whose names begin with the letter shown.

Home Activity: Ask your child to make rhyming words for *y* (*barn—yarn, lawn—yawn*).

Name ______________________

Color.

I. y

2. y

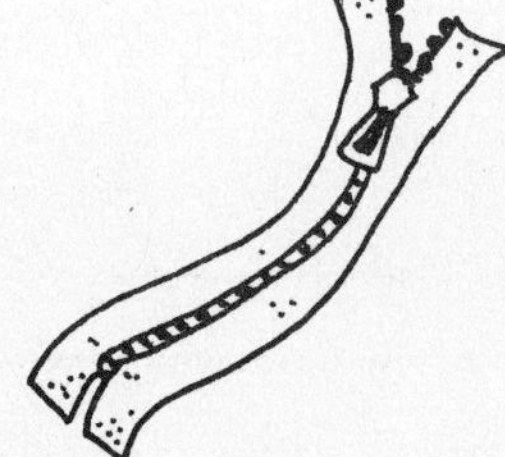

3. y

Directions: In each row, color the picture that begins with the letter shown.

Home Activity: Help your child make up two-word phrases with words that begin with *y—yellow yarn.*

Name ____________________

Draw lines.

Yy

Yy

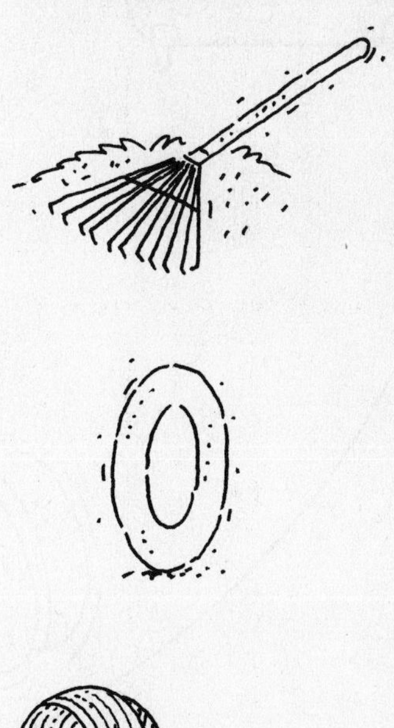

Directions: Draw lines from the letters to the pictures that begin with that sound.

Home Activity: Say a word (*yard, yellow, yam*) and have your child name the letter for the beginning sound.

Name ______________________________

Draw lines.

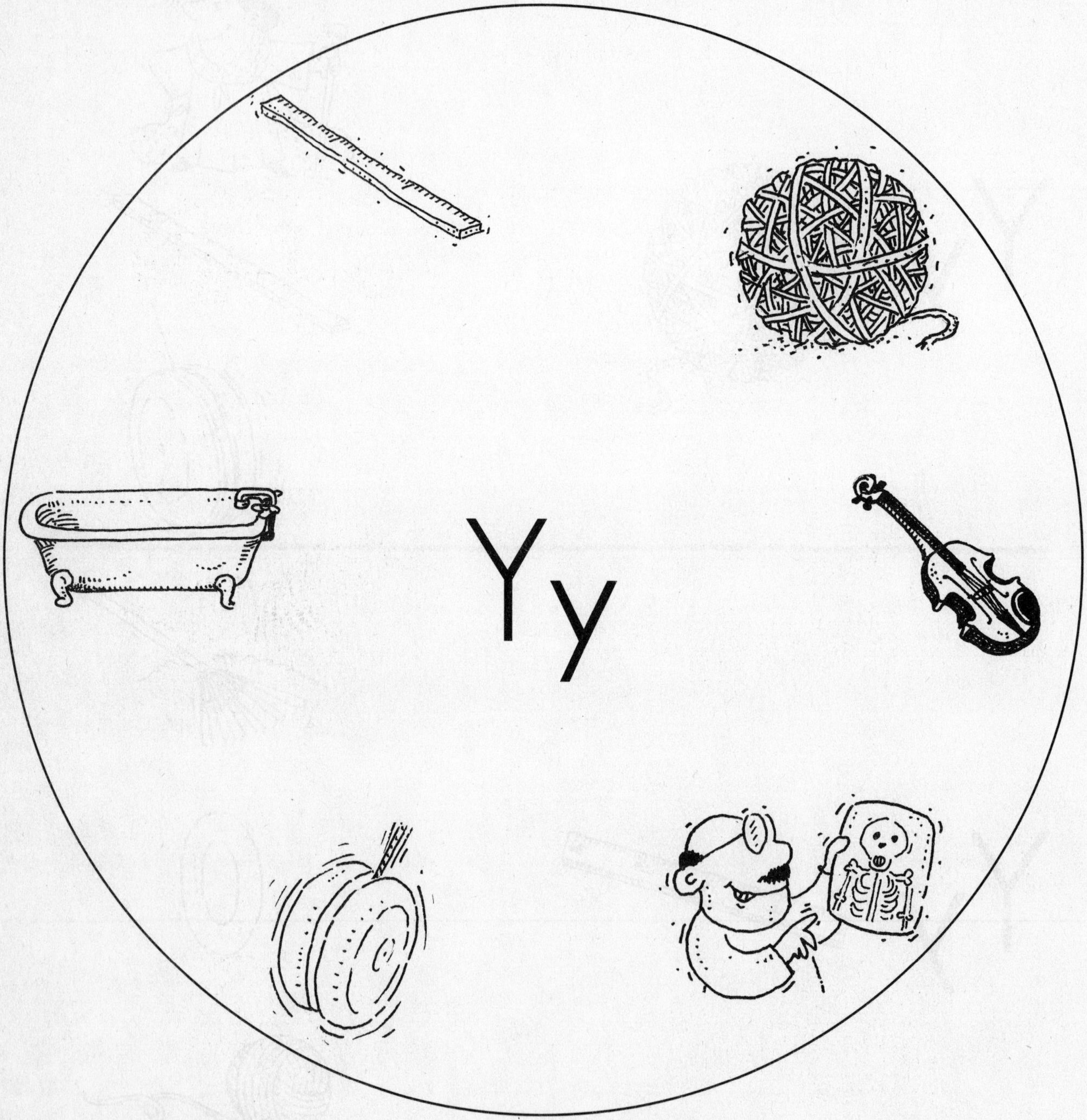

Yy

Directions: Draw lines connecting the letters in the middle with the pictures on the circle that begins with *y*.

Home Activity: Say a picture name and have your child write the letter for the beginning sound.

Name ______________________________

Circle.

Zz

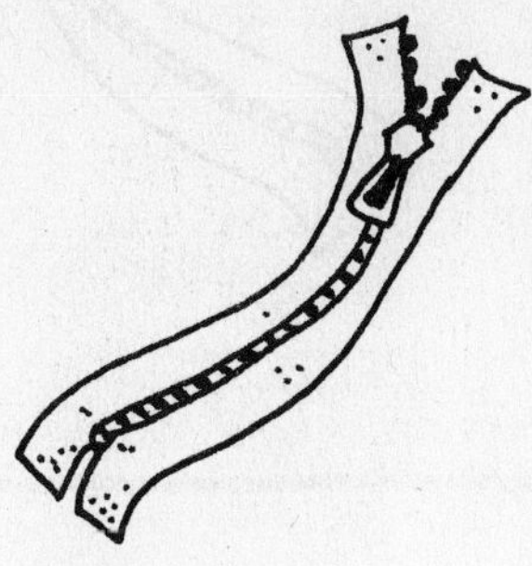

Directions: Circle the pictures whose names begin like *zebra*.

Home Activity: Point to *z* and have your child name a word that begins with that letter.

Name ________________________________

Circle.

1. z

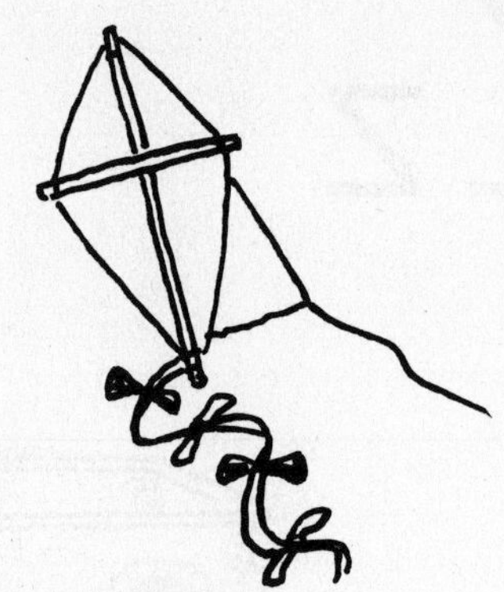

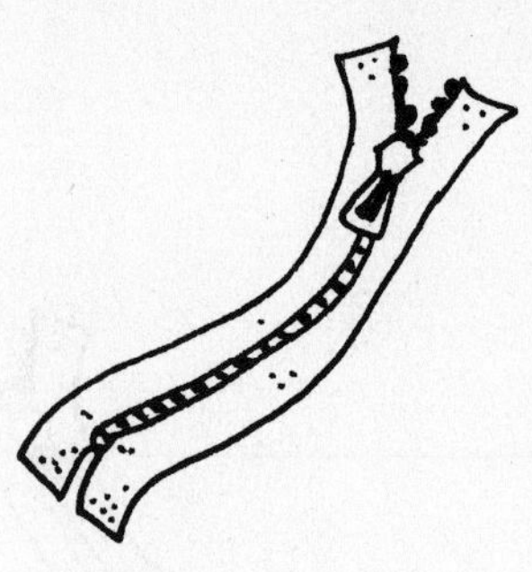

2. z

3. z

Directions: In each row, circle the word that begins with *z*.

Home Activity: Say a word. Have your child write the first letter of the word.

Name ______________________________

Circle.

Z z

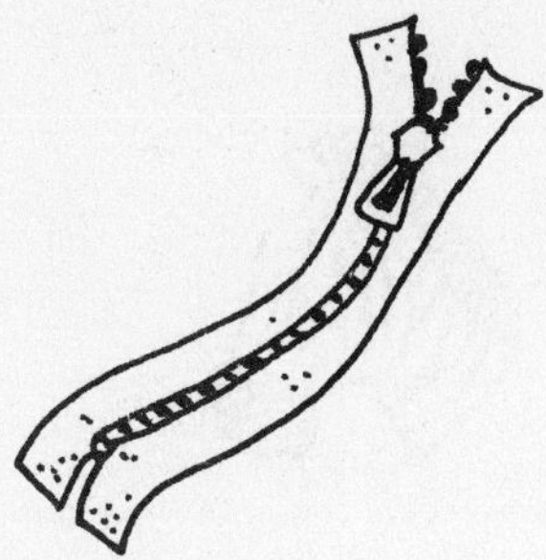

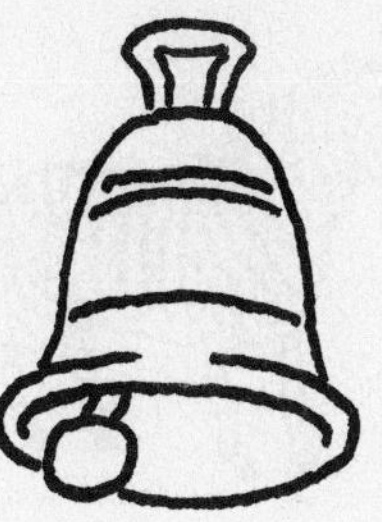

Directions: Color the pictures that begin with *z*.

Home Activity: Help your child make up two-word phrases that begin with *z—zippy zebras.*

Name ________________________________

Draw lines.

Zz 

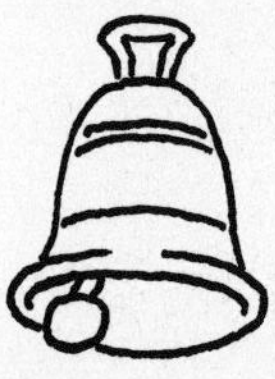

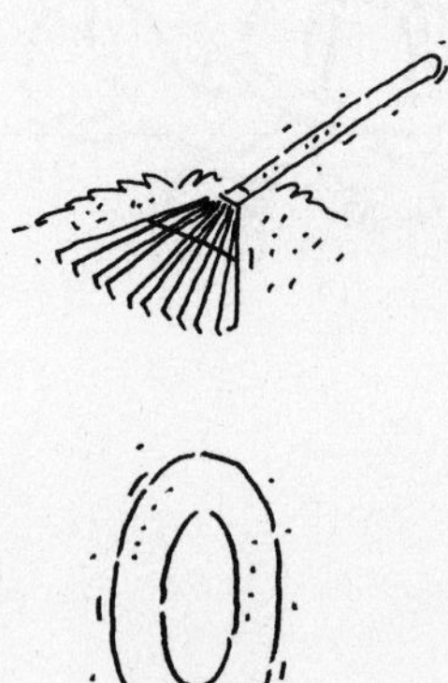

Zz 

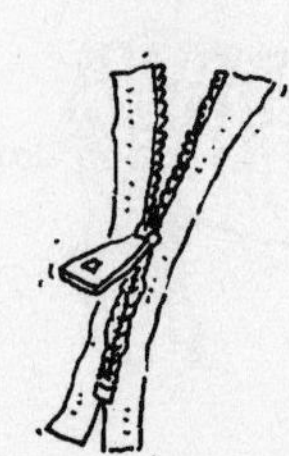

Directions: In each row, draw lines from the letters to the pictures that begin with *z*.

Home Activity: As you say different words, have your child identify the ones that start with *z*.

Name ______________________________

Draw lines.

Zz

Directions: Draw lines connecting the letters in the middle with the pictures on the circle that begin with *z*.

Home Activity: Say a picture name and have your child write the letter for the beginning sound.

Name ____________________

Color.

sun 

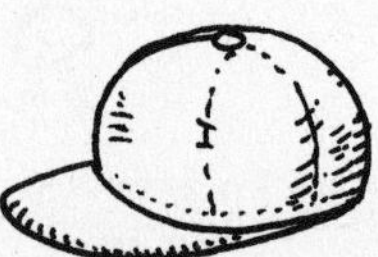

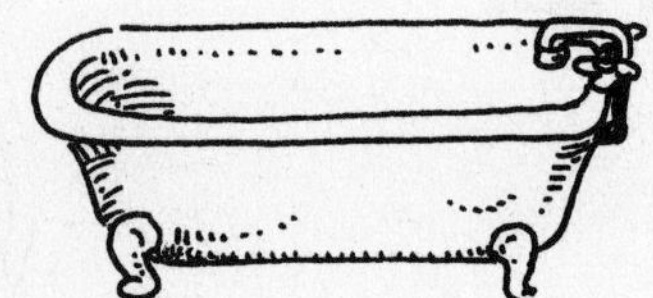

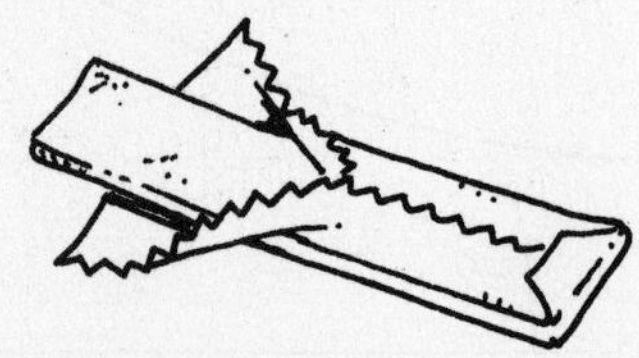

Directions: Color the pictures whose names have the short *u* sound.

Home Activity: Have your child name other words with the short *u* sound.

Name ______________________

Draw a line.

1.

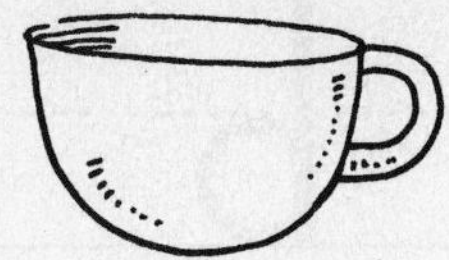

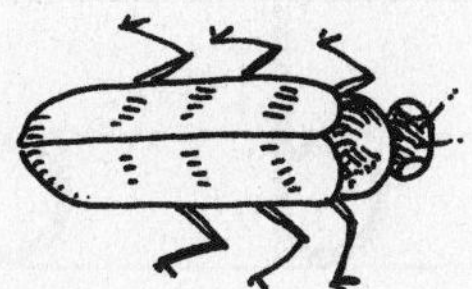

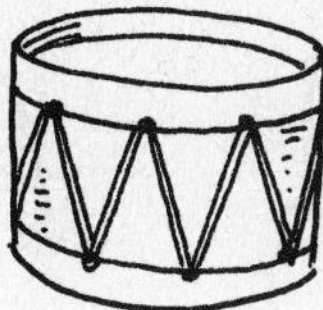

2.

3.

4.

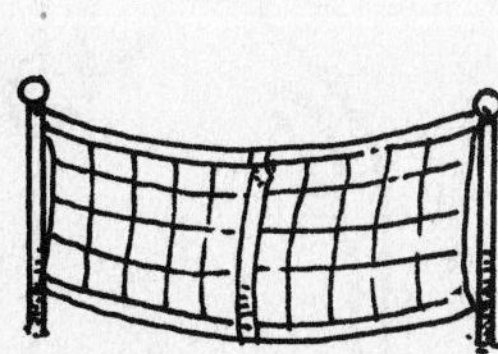

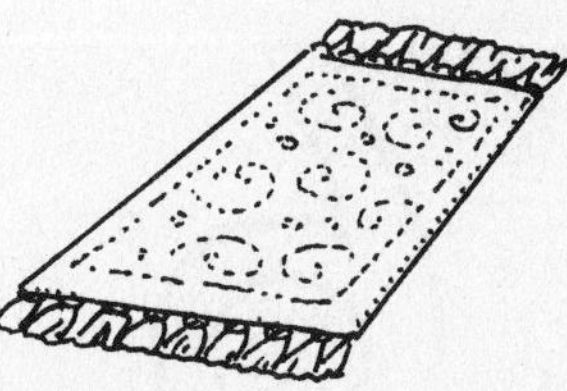

Directions: Draw a line to match the pictures with the short *u* sound.

Home Activity: Have your child name words that rhyme with *bug*—*mug, rug, tug, hug, lug, dug, jug.*

Name ______________________

Circle.

1.

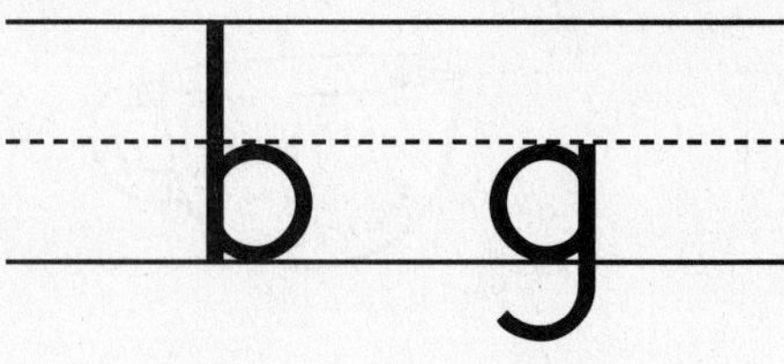

2.

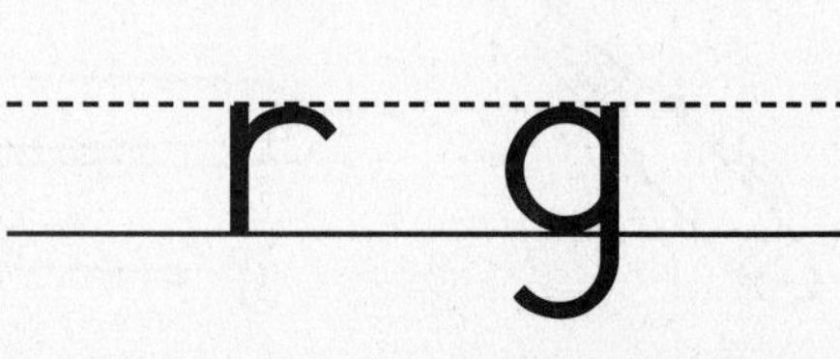

3.

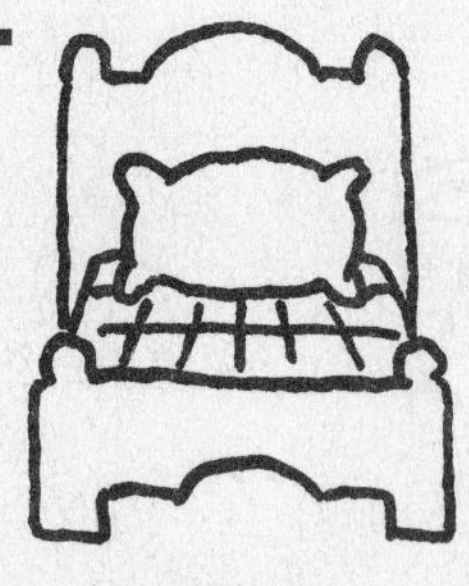

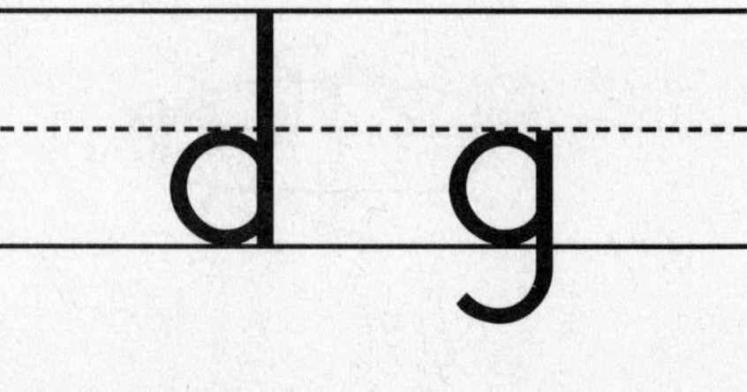

4.

Directions: In each row, circle the picture with the short *u* sound. Write the letter to finish the picture name.

Home Activity: Make letter cards for *b, r, d, j, g,* and *u*. Help your child arrange the letters to make the words on this page.

Name ______________________________

Color.

1.

cut

2.

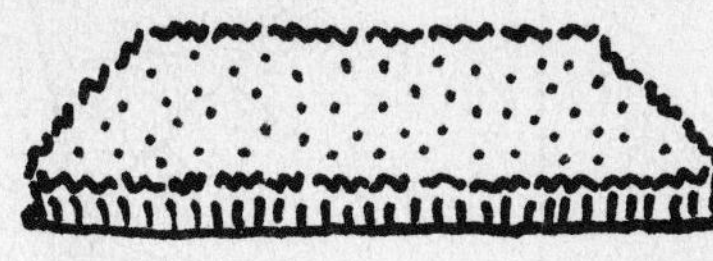

rug

3.

up

4.

duck

Directions: In each box, color the picture that rhymes with the word at the top of the box.

Home Activity: Write the word *cut* on a sheet of paper. Help your child write words that rhyme with *cut*.

Name ______________________________

Circle.

1. rug

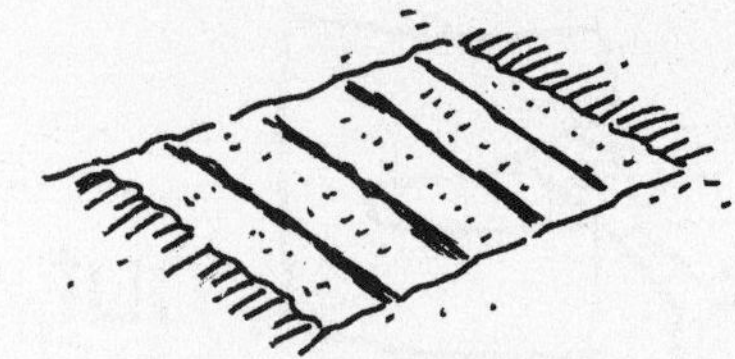

2. bug

3. jug

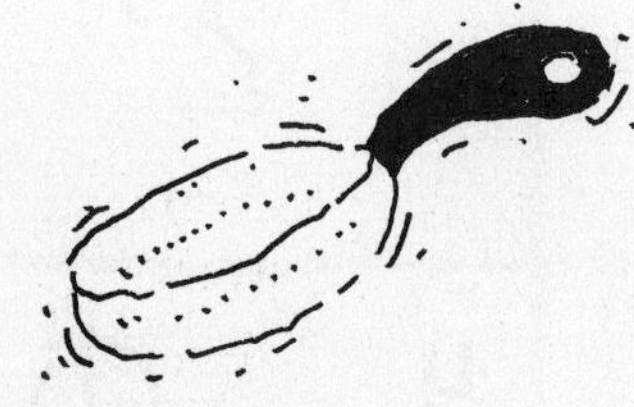

4. cup

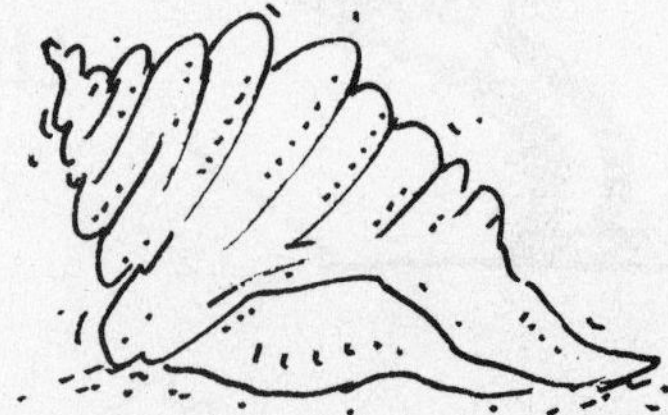

5. cut

Directions: In each row, circle the picture the word names.

Home Activity: Point to a word on the page and have your child use the word in a sentence.

Name ______________________________

Circle.

1. 

Mm

 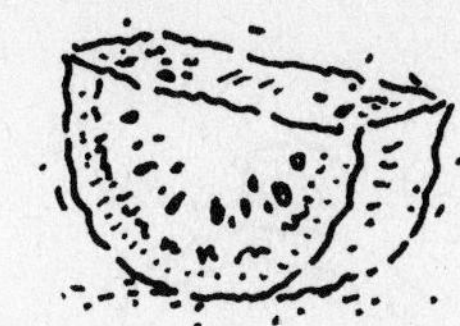 

2. 

Rr

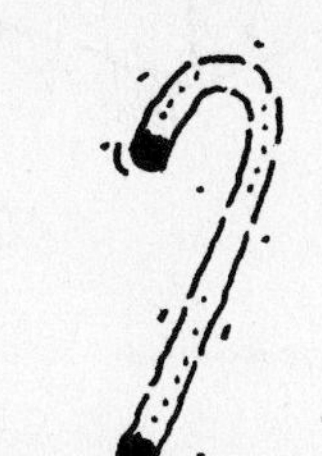  

3. 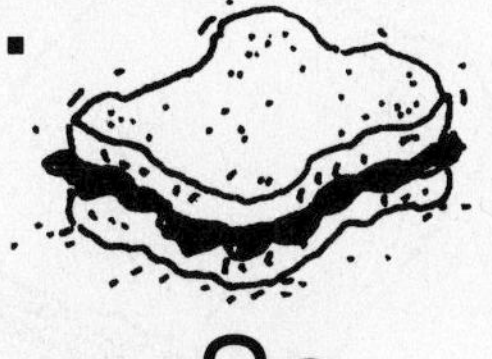

Ss

4. 

Mm

5. 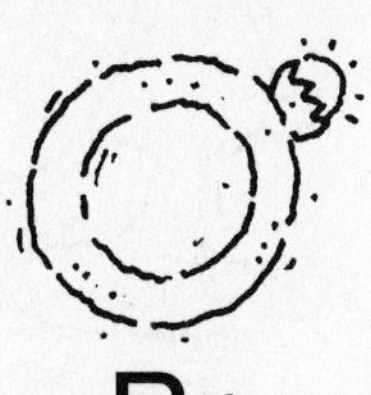

Rr

Directions: In each row, circle the picture that begins with the letter shown in the first box.

Home Activity: Say words beginning with *m*, *r*, and *s* and have your child identify the beginning letter in each.

Name ______________________

Color.

1. Bb

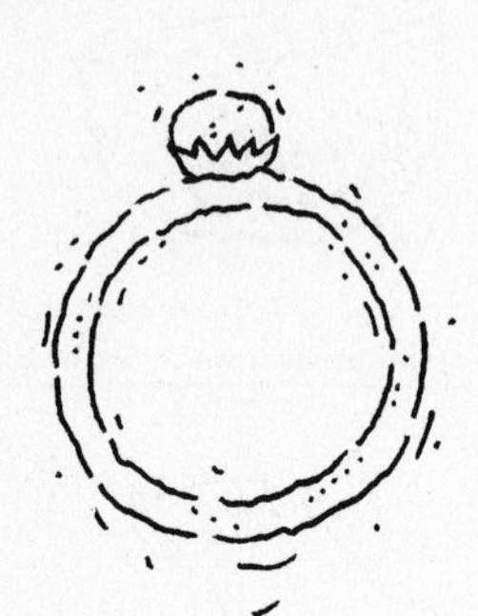

2. Tt

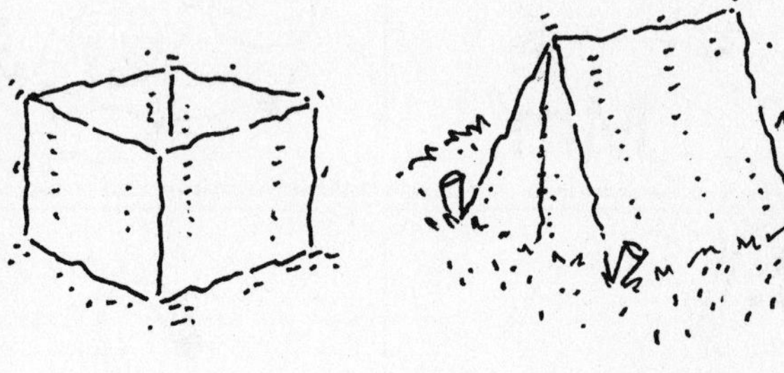

3. Ff

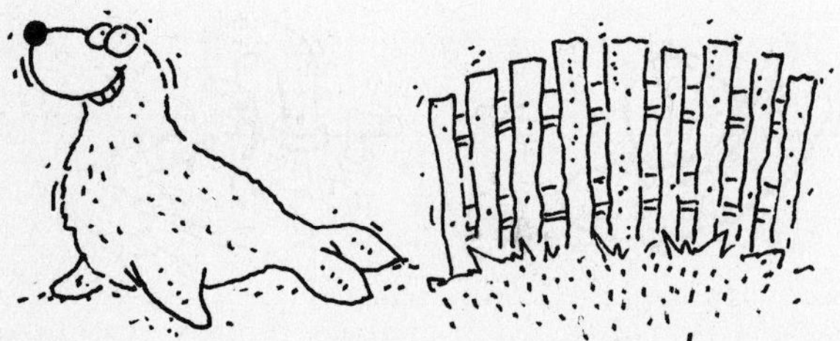

4. Nn

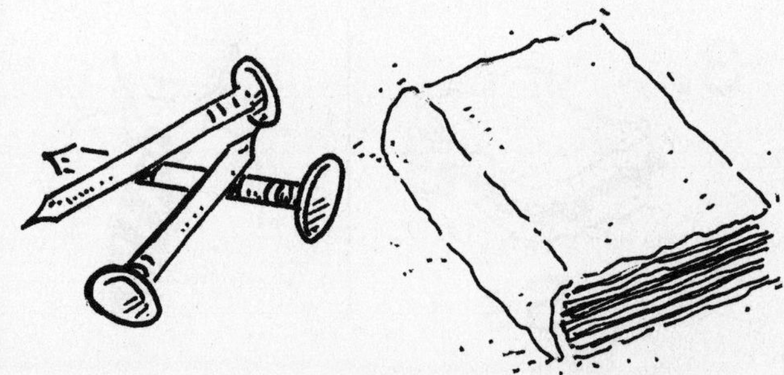

5. Tt

6. Ff

Directions: In each box, color the picture that begins with the letter at the top of the box.

Home Activity: Say a picture name and have your child tell the letter for the beginning sound.

Name ______________________________

Color.

1. Pp

2. Gg

3. Hh

4. Pp

5. Gg

6. Hh

Directions: In each box, color the picture that begins with the letter at the top of the box.

Home Activity: Say a picture name and ask your child to name the letter for the beginning sound.

Name ______________________________

Circle.

1. 

c d l

2. 

k l d

3. 

k l d

4. 

c d l

5. 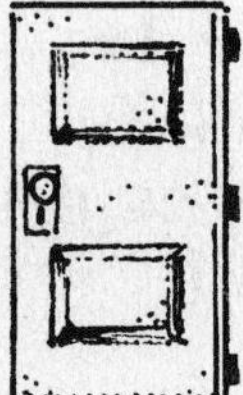

c d l

6. 

k l d

7. 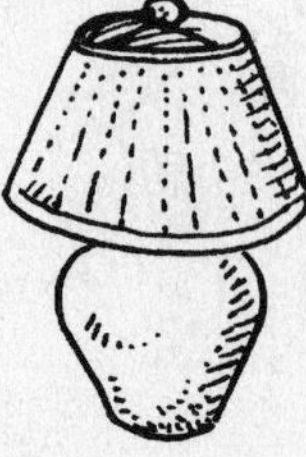

k l d

8. 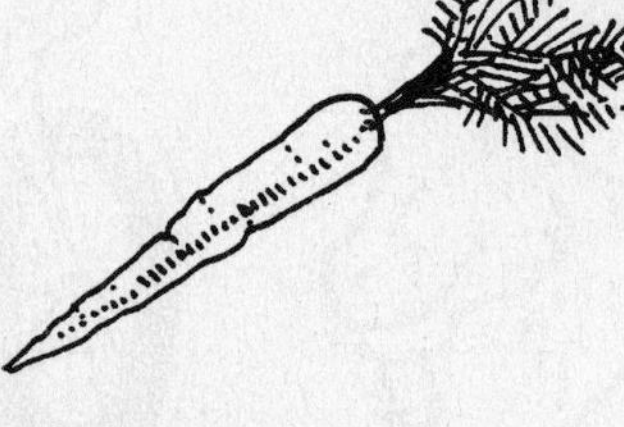

c d l

Directions: In each box, circle the letter that begins the picture name.

Home Activity: Look through magazines and books for pictures of things that begin with *c, d, l,* and *k*.

Name ______________________

Circle.

1. 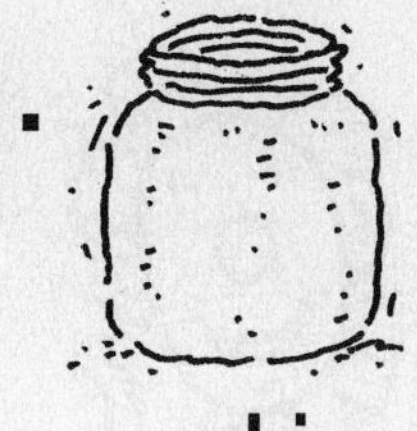 Jj | 

2. 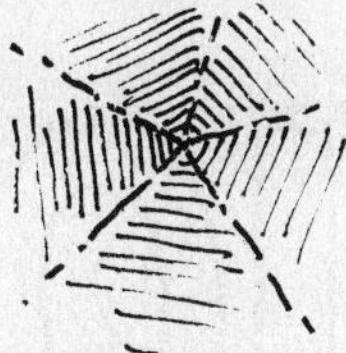 Ww | 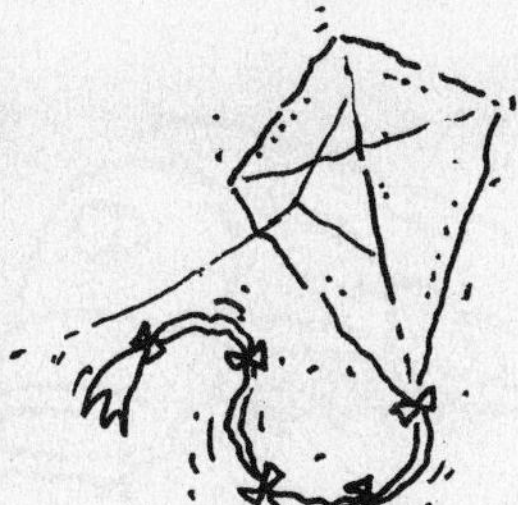  

3.  Vv |   

4.  Qq |   

5.  Ww | 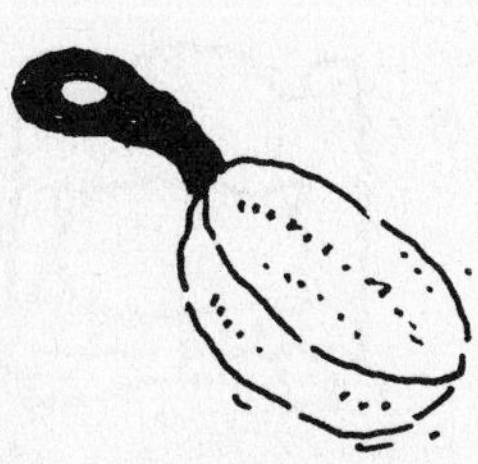 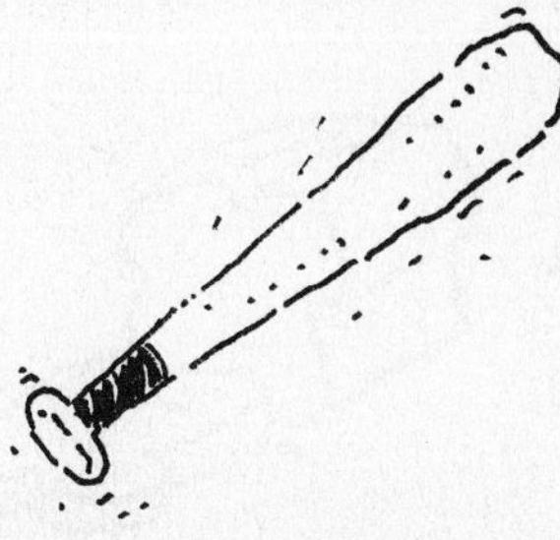

Directions: In each row, circle the picture that begins with the letter shown in the first box.

Home Activity: Say several words beginning with *j, w, v,* and *q* and have your child identify the beginning letter in each word.

Name ______________________

Circle.

1.    

2.    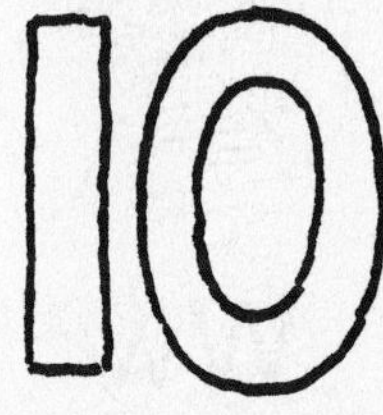

3. 

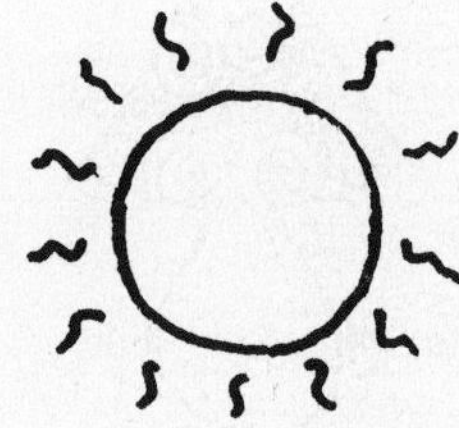 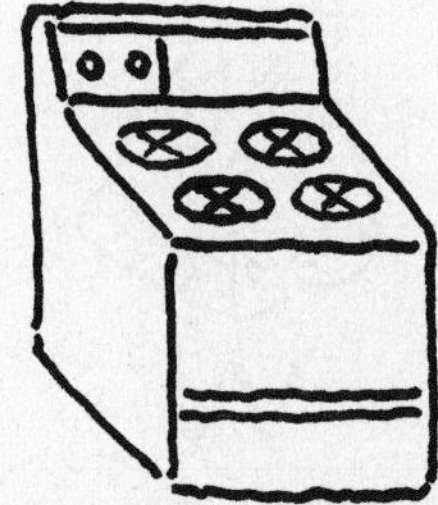

4.    

5.  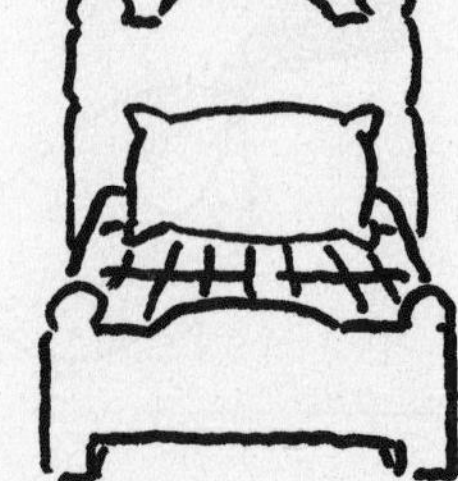 

Directions: In each row, circle the pictures that begin the same.

Home Activity: Have your child make up a silly phrase using words that begin with *cl, tr, st, gl,* or *br*.

Name ______________________________

Draw a line.

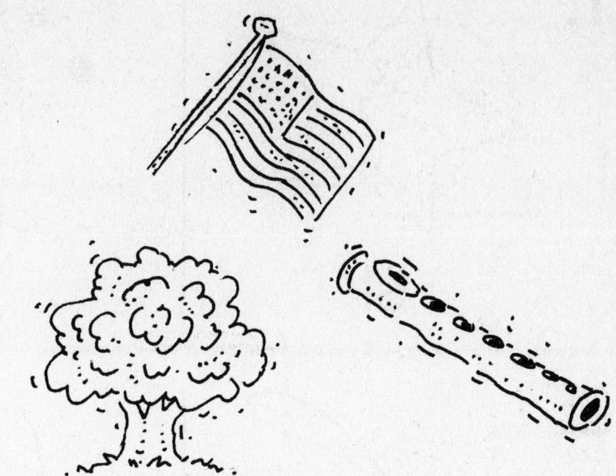

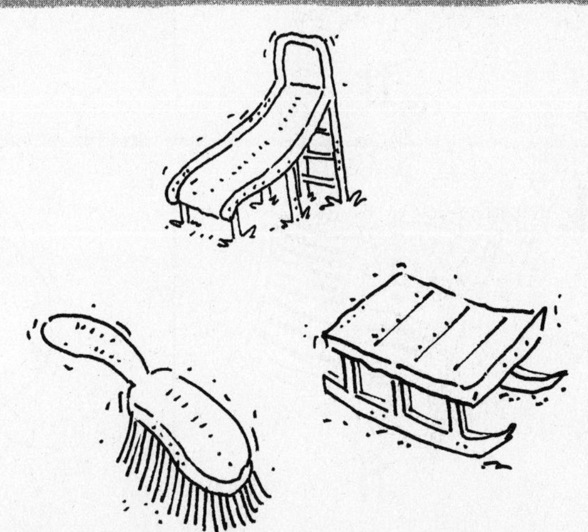

Directions: Draw lines between the pictures that begin alike.

Home Activity: Ask your child to draw pictures of other things that begin with *dr, fl, bl, gr, cl,* and *sl.*

Name ______________________________

Color.

1.

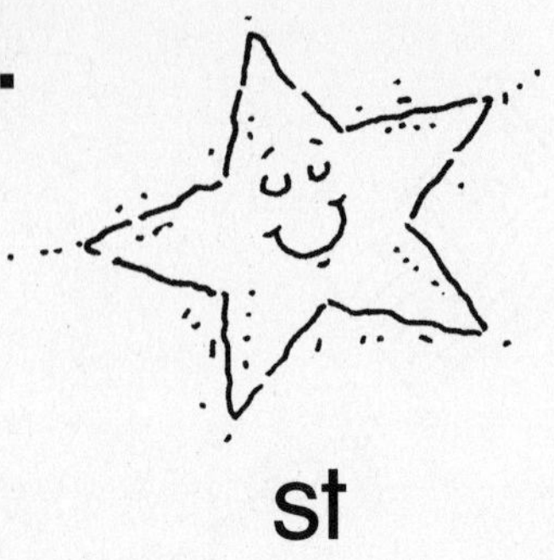

st

2.

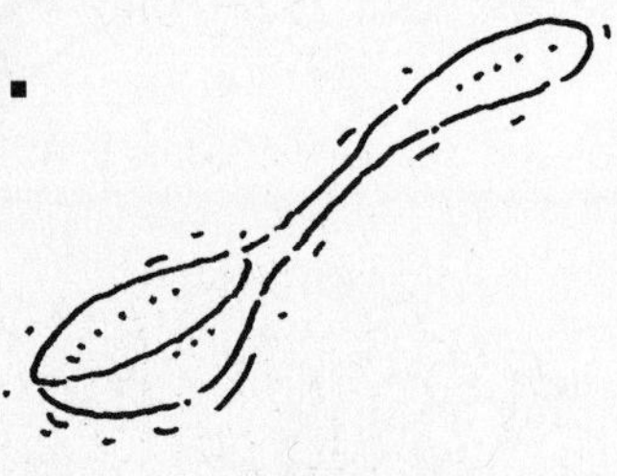

sp

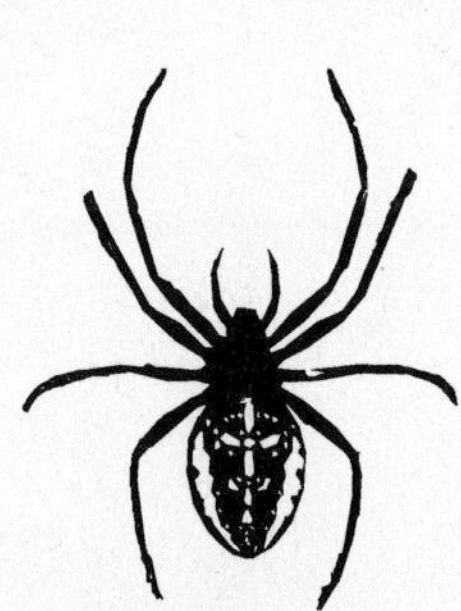

3.

tr

4.

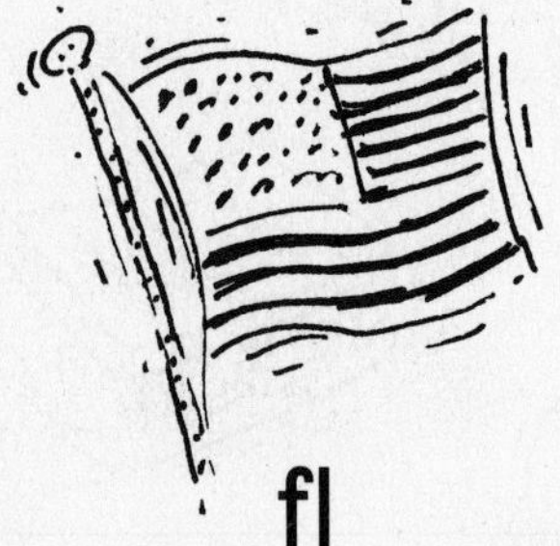

fl

Directions: In each row, color the picture that begins like the first picture.

Home Activity: Have your child look in magazines or newspapers for pictures of things that begin with *st*, *sp*, *tr*, and *fl*.

Name ____________________

Draw lines.

s		b	
st		bl	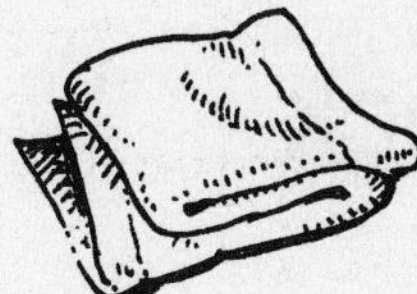
f	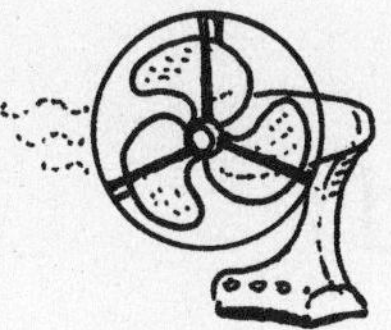	c	
fl	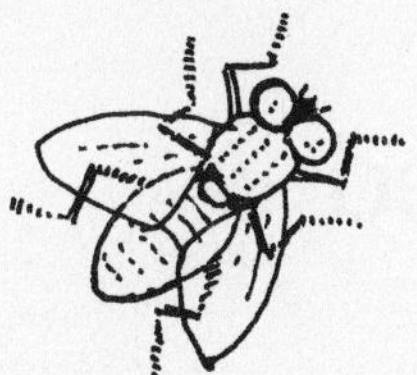	cr	
d		t	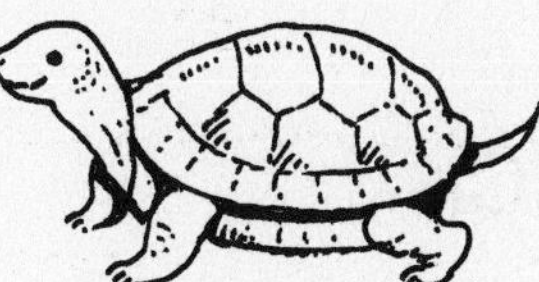
dr		tr	

Directions: Draw lines to match the letters with the pictures.

Home Activity: Have your child make up a sentence using the two words from each box on the page.

Name ______________________________

Draw lines.

lock		hop	
clock		stop	
tack		bed	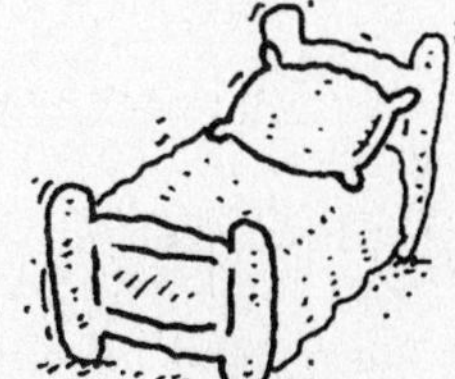
track		sled	
duck		bag	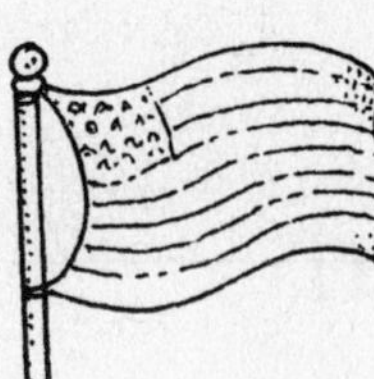
truck		flag	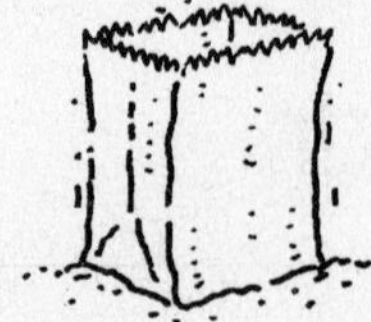

Directions: Draw lines to match the words with the pictures.

Home Activity: Have your child think of words that rhyme with words on this page. Draw pictures to go with them.

Name ______________________________

Color.

1\.

cat

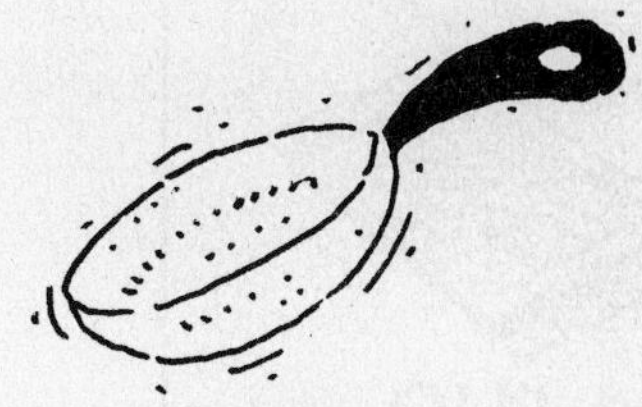

2\.

bed

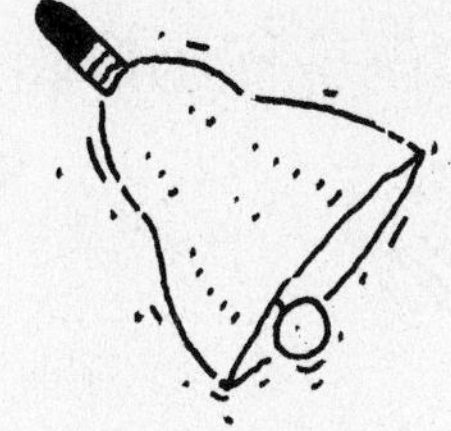

3\.

pig

4\.

fox

5\.

sun

Directions: In each row, color the picture with the same vowel sound as the first word.

Home Activity: Say one of the words on the page and help your child write the word.

Name ______________________________

Color.

1.

rug

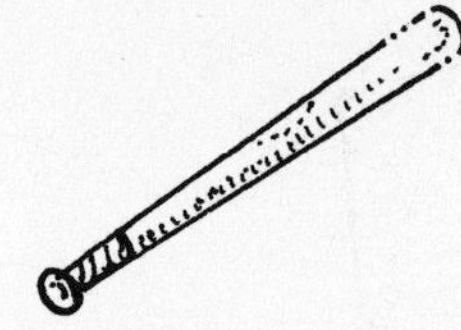

2.

big

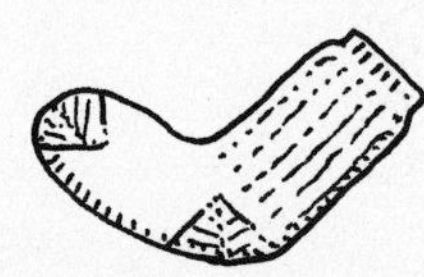

3.

hop

4.

hen

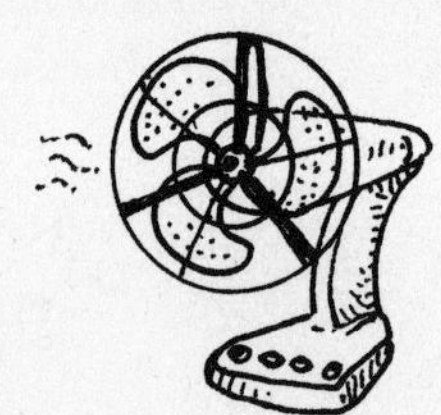

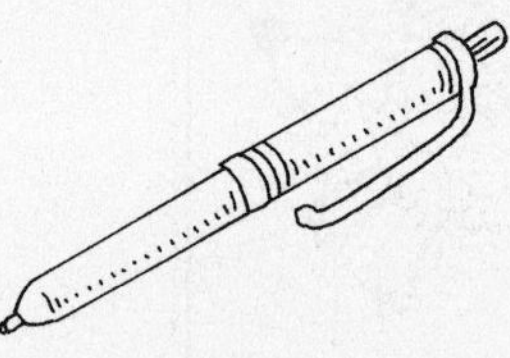

5.

rat

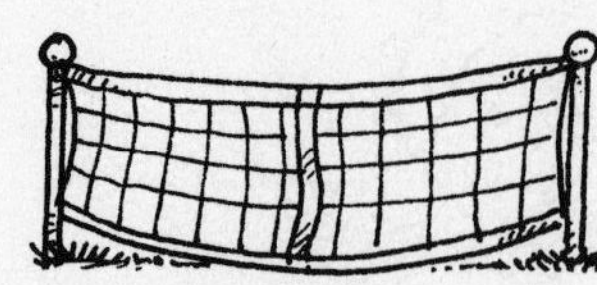

Directions: In each row, color the picture that rhymes with the first word.

Home Activity: Write *an* and have your child add a beginning letter to make a word. Continue with *it* and *up*.

Name ________________________________

Circle.

1.  hot hop

2.  bib bit

3.  cap can

4. 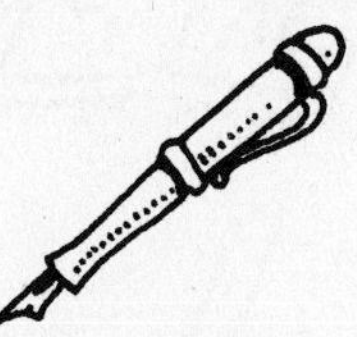 pen pet

5.  hut hug

Directions: In each row, circle the word that names the picture.

Home Activity: Have your child think of several words that rhyme with *hop, pen,* and *hut*.

Name ______________________________

Draw lines.

hat

hit

cut

cat

bug

bag

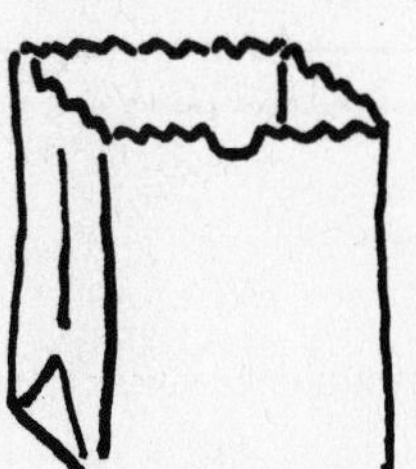

mop

map

Directions: Draw lines to match the words with the pictures.

Home Activity: Have your child use the words on the page in sentences.

Name ________________________

Write.

1\.

2\.

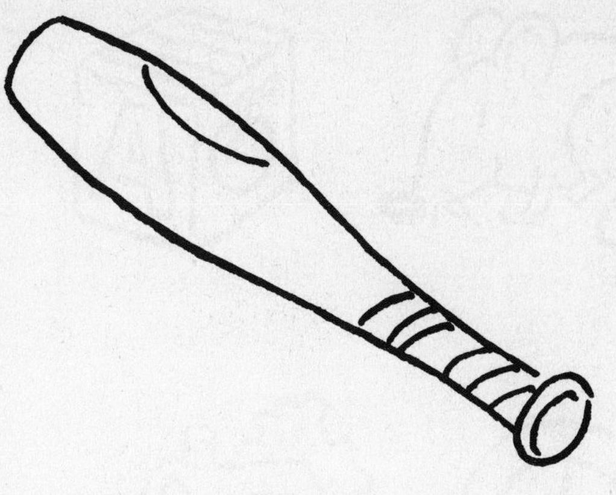

3\.

4\.

Directions: Write the word that names the picture.

Home Activity: Have your child write words such as the following: *red, fed, hat, cat, rug, dug, dig, big.*

Name ______________________________

Skill Review

Draw lines.

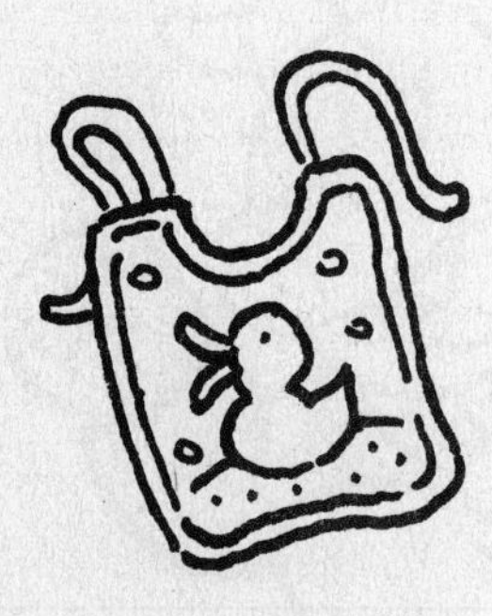

Directions: Draw lines connecting the pictures whose names rhyme.

Home Activity: Recite nursery rhymes and ask your child to name rhyming words.

Name ________________________

Circle.

1.    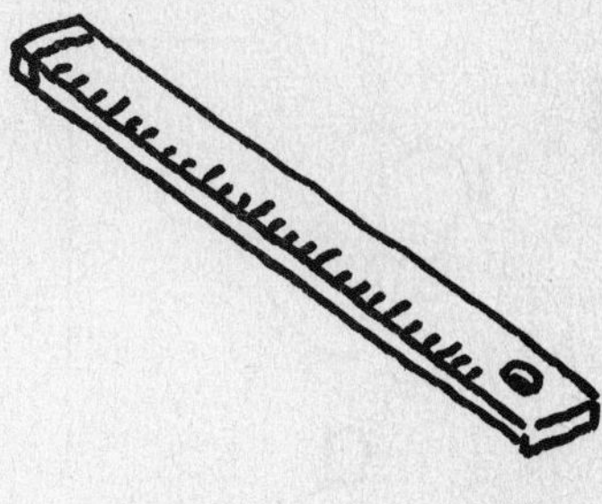

2.  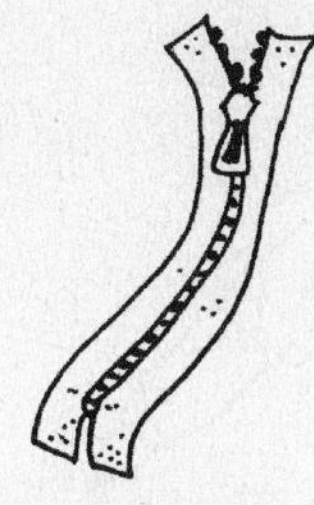  

3. 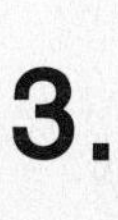   

4.  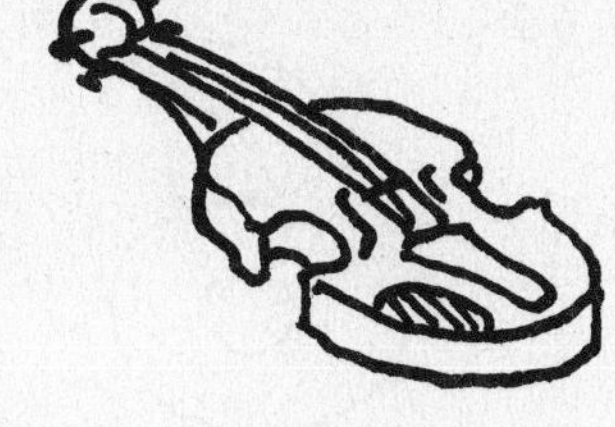  

5.    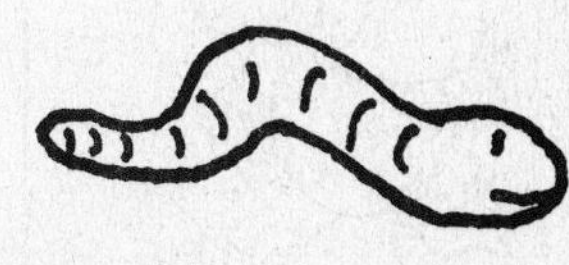

Directions: In each row, circle the pictures that begin with the same sound as the first picture.

Home Activity: Say a picture name and have your child name a word that begins with the same sound.

Name ______________________

Circle.

1. 
a

2. 
e

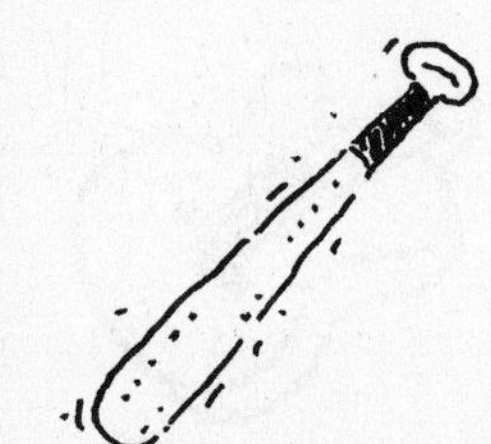  

3. 
i

  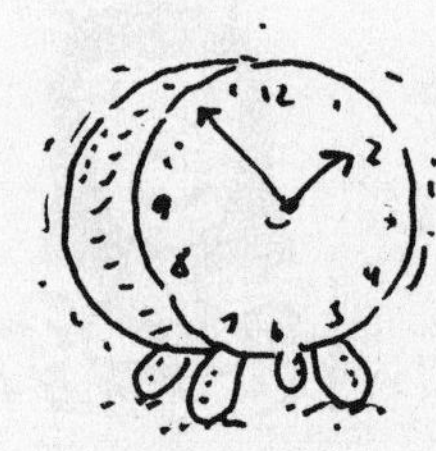

4. 
o

  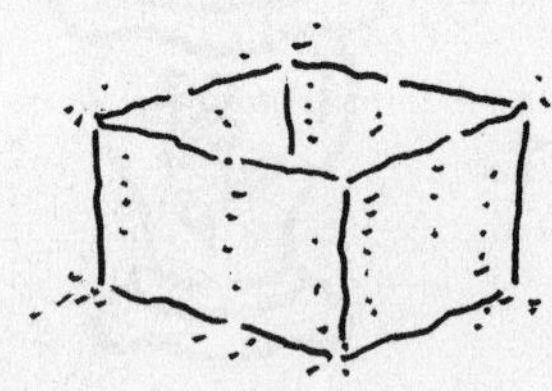

5. 
u

Directions: In each row, circle the pictures that have the same vowel sound as the picture in the first box.

Home Activity: Say a picture name and have your child name the letter for the vowel sound.

Name ______________________

Color.

1.

st

2.

bl

3.

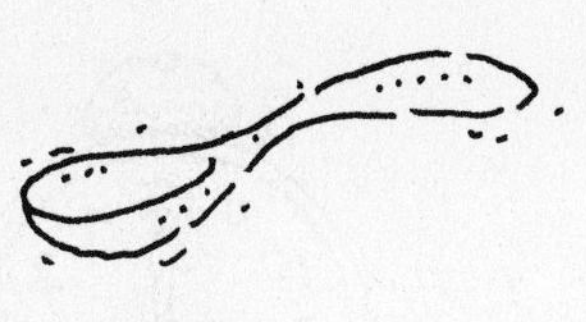

sp

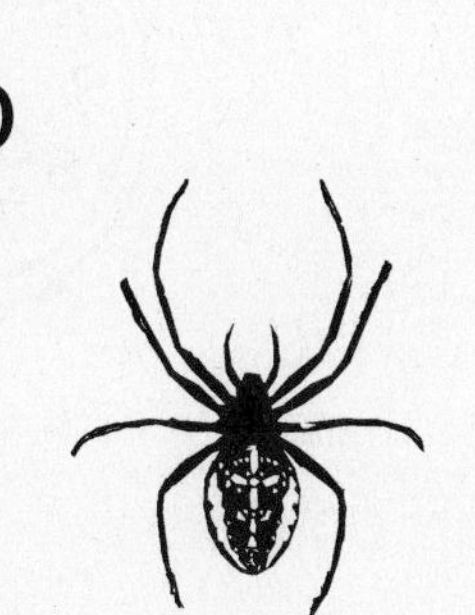

4.

dr

5.

fl

6.

gr

Directions: In each box, color the picture that begin with the letters in the box.

Home Activity: Have your child point to a picture and name other words that begin the same.

Name ______________________________

Circle.

1.

b bl br

2.

s st sl

3.

f fl fr

4.

c cl cr

5.

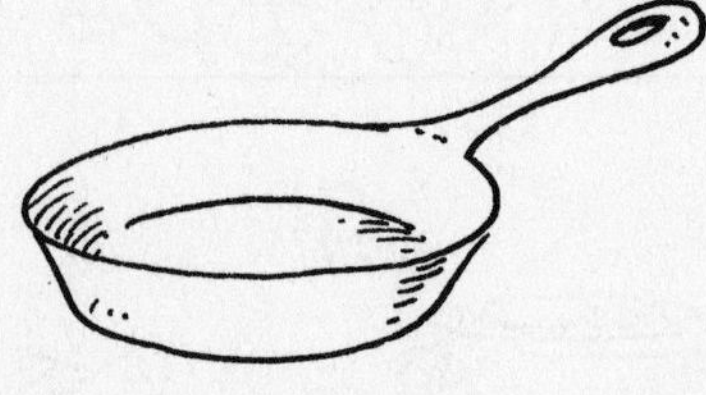

p pl pr

6.

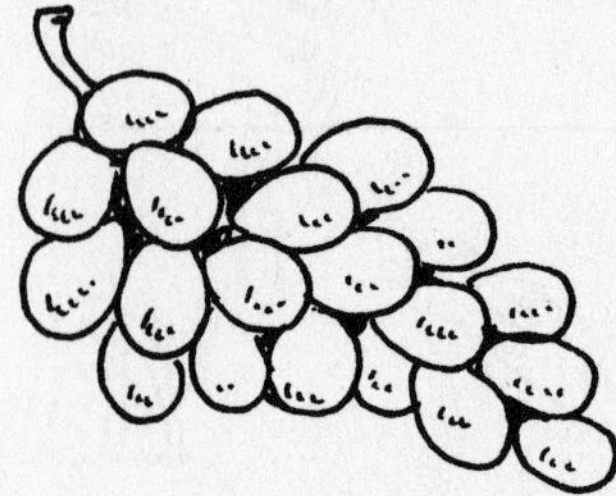

g gl gr

Directions: In each box, circle the letters that begin the picture name.

Home Activity: Read a sentence from a book. Have your child identify the beginning letter for some of the words.